The Crack in the Wall

The Crack in the Wall

Gisela Selo

Marylou Selo, project manager

Bergamot Books
bergamotbooks.com
Gail Spilsbury, publisher
Katie Sherman, senior editor, interior design
Leslie Dickersin, cover design

ISBN 978-1-7354275-2-2

Cover photograph: Gisela Selo as Madame Butterfly
Insert: Portrait of young Gisela Selo

Table of Contents

Foreword

One night in the early 1980's, my phone rang while I was reading in bed. "Hello, this is Gisela Selo, is this Marylou Selo?" The name Gisela Selo did not ring a bell with me. But it turned out that Gisela was my second cousin. She had gone to the German consulate to obtain a certified translation of her inheritance documents.

The receptionist gave her my business card, because I am registered as a translator and interpreter with the consulate. Gisela could not believe the translator had the same last name as her own. During that late-night phone chat, we established that our grandfathers were brothers. She was descended from the eldest brother and I from the youngest. Given that there were seventeen children in our grandfathers' nuclear family, it came as no surprise that Gisela and I had a twenty-year age difference.

Gisela's German father, Herbert Louis Selo had a bad reputation in the family, and hence I had never been made aware of his family when I came to the United States in 1963.

But Gisela was close to another relative in New York— Klare Selo, Her aunt Klare was the widow of Richard Selo, who had died young. Their daughter Margaret lives in Connecticut, and Gisela and Margaret saw a lot of each other when Margaret was still single and living in Queens.

While Gisela's history is in part a Holocaust story, as she and her father escaped Nazi persecution and the death camps mine is not, though my father, Werner Selo, also fled Germany, in 1933, and settled for more than a decade in Bolivia, where he met and married my Bolivian mother, Paz. Thus Gisela and I both have Jewish fathers and Catholic mothers..

I was born in Bolivia, and grew up from age nine in Amsterdam—where Gisela also lived briefly before the outbreak of World War II. I went to university in Geneva and afterward worked in the United States at the Library of Congress and also as contractor for the United States Department of State, using my fluency in five languages as an interpreter—Dutch, German, English, French, and Spanish.

Gisela lived in Howard Beach at the time we met, some distance from my home on the Upper West Side. We only saw each other a couple of times a year, but also had many late-night phone visits. Gisela was living with her partner Chris at the time, a member of the Cosa Nostra. He was the nicest guy and treated women like queens, going out of his way to please them. Numerous times he picked me up at the airport after my business trips to Europe and drove me home. He would not have family of Gisela on public transportation late at night. I loved to listen to his stories and to know that if ever harm should come to me, he would take care of the evil-doer, as I was now "family."

When Gisela turned eighty, she moved into assisted living near the World Trade Center. She so enjoyed being back in Manhattan with all the cultural resources it offered. But financial issues dictated that she move to a more modest facility. The Carnegie, at 96th Street and Second Avenue, close to the 96th Street Y and the museums, became her home. Now it was easier for me to visit her and to accompany her on outings. She was always immensely grateful for these times together. A highlight came when she turned ninety and my flutist friend Hendrik from Holland happened to be in town. He agreed to present a shortened solo performance of Mozart's *Magic Flute* for Gisela and her friends. It was a great success, and Gisela was the talk of the home for weeks.

Gisela had a rough but rich life. Amazingly, she fully found herself only after her eightieth birthday. Being taken away from her loving mother at age five, and not being wanted or loved by her father, she buried her feelings under layers of self-protection, "The Wall" as Gisela deemed it. A wonderful therapist, Amour, and her relationship with Chris, helped her reconnect to her inner feelings. After retiring from the jewelry business—one of her many enterprises—she had time to paint and exhibit, to sing and perform, and to write poetry and work on the memoir she had dreamed of writing. She enjoyed community and forged many friendships—most notably the friendship she developed later in life with Phyllis, the daughter of a Rabbi. On the occasion of another cousin of our fathers', our Uncle Rudi's ninetieth birthday, we flew to San Francisco to celebrate with that branch of the Selo family: cousins Elaine Selo and Richard Selo and Richard's family. Gisela had mellowed out from her difficult years and was able to enjoy the family's acceptance and love.

In 2019, Gisela's failing eyesight and hearing required her

to move to a nursing home. Margaret and I cleaned out her apartment on Second Avenue. Among many little treasures we found chapters of this book scattered in different places. There were several versions of the important chapters. There were also manilla envelopes containing photographs pertaining to the chapters. I gathered all the material into a suitcase and copied to a flash-drive all the memoir writing we could find on her computer.

Ironically, Coronavirus brought new safety measures to the nursing home and plunged Gisela into isolation once again. She who had suffered loneliness and had done so much to avoid it now was not allowed visitors to give her the warmth and love she craved.

Never did I imagine how much time and detailed work goes into shaping and producing a cohesive a book from this patchwork of memories. And of course, many details are missing, are unknown, such as dates or revelatory correspondence between her father or other close relatives.

My gratitude is immense to those who helped during the publishing process of Gisela's book. Katharine Sherman undertook the painstaking job of editing and stitching together in a more understandable chronology the chapters and bits and pieces that I found on Gisela's computer and around her apartment. Gail Spilsbury of Bergamot Books provided publishing guidance and further editorial work. Without her none of this would have happened! Leslie Dickersin made a beautiful cover, capturing Gisela's inner grace and musical passion. I, myself, took on the task of sifting through hundreds of Gisela's photographs and narrowing down a selection for the book.

Bringing *The Crack in the Wall* to print has been a unique and collaborative experience. Most of all it has created a great joy and satisfaction in me to know that Gisela's challenging and remarkable life has been preserved, and that this memoir can be shared with many people who will relate to her many travails and triumphs.

Marylou Selo

It Started with Asparagus

Noon. As always, my father came upstairs to for family dinner. Today we had fresh asparagus. He watched me as I chewed on a rubbery stalk. Before heading back downstairs he warned me, "Your mouth had better be empty when I get back."

Well, it wasn't gone. I hadn't found a way to discretely dispose of the asparagus. Anna, the housekeeper, was watching me carefully. I suppose she was still trying to figure out how I'd managed to get rid of an entire plate of spinach the week before—out the window.

My father returned upstairs for dessert, and when he saw that I was still chewing, he grew enraged. An initial threat ensued: "I'm going down to see another patient, and when I come back, you'd better be finished!"

He was gone for quite a while, but the longer I chewed, the more impossible the asparagus became to swallow. I cringed when I heard his footsteps on the stairs. He saw that I was still chewing, and without a word he grabbed me by the collar. With a flashlight in his hand, he pushed me down several flights of stairs and I fell into the coal cellar, He firmly sat me down on a wooden crate. When I started to cry, he made another threat. "Stop your sniveling. You will stay here until you finish, even if it takes all night."

He took the flashlight, pounded up the stairs, and locked the coal cellar door behind him. I was left in pitch darkness, petrified, feeling very small—I was only five years old.

Gradually, my eyes grew accustomed to the dark. I began to make out shapes in the blackness. Most disturbingly, a large gaping mouth appeared, ready to swallow me—the cellar furnace. Furtively I stared at that furnace. There was a growing mound of coal in front of it, but otherwise, the nothing of stillness filled the cellar. I stopped crying, slid off the wooden crate, and inched forward until I reached the edge of the pile. I took the chewy wad of asparagus out of my mouth, pushed it deeply into the coal, and dusted out any remaining evidence with my foot. My heart was pounding; the coal kept shifting.

What if I were buried under the pile and no one ever found me? I thought. I stood very still. Finally the coal stopped moving. I backed up gingerly until my legs reached the wooden crate, and I sat down again. An overwhelming sense of triumph came over me. The asparagus was gone! I wiped my dirty hands on the underside of my smock, but figured that my black shoes and stockings disguise the coal dust.

I waited in that dark cellar for what seemed like hours, feeling alone and abandoned. Why doesn't Mutti come? I kept thinking. Daddy doesn't care about me at all. I think he hates me.

Finally, I heard the key turn in the lock of the cellar door.

"Well, are you finished?"

Appropriately obedient on the outside, but inwardly triumphant, I answered, "Yes, Daddy."

"Hmm," he muttered suspiciously. He shone his flashlight over the floor and the pile of coal, and not finding any trace of the asparagus, he led me back up the stairs into daylight.

Early Memories

I was rudely awakened during the night by Sister Margaret, who was trying to get me up and dressed. As she gathered my belongings together, she said cheerfully, "Someone is waiting for you."

I rubbed my sleepy eyes and thought, Oh, good, that's Mutti coming to get me like she promised.

But it wasn't Mutti. It was my father and his sister, my Aunt Gerda. Aunt Gerda took me by the hand and said kindly, "We're going to Grossmama's."

"Where is Mutti?"

"Your Mutti?" My father grumbled. "Your Mutti doesn't want you anymore."

I shut up—silenced in confusion.

My parents were divorced when I was three. According to the German divorce laws at the time, the guilty party, in this case my mother, lost custody. Yet, for my first five years I had been living with her. Those five years draw a blank in my memory; I remember absolutely nothing. My earliest conscious vision is the Catholic orphanage where my mother hid me upon learning from the cleaning woman that my father was looking for me. One of the priests had assured her that the Church would not give me up to my Jewish father. But here he was. With my free hand, I pushed my doll carriage along the cobbled street. It started to rain. Suddenly, one wheel came off and rolled down the street. My father, annoyed, threw the whole carriage onto a pile of garbage, ignoring my screams that my favorite doll was asleep inside. I can't recall much else, except that I cried for a long time that night.

I had never been to the home of my grandmother, or Grossmama as I affectionately called her. While my Grosspapa was alive, Mutti and I were not allowed in his house, but he had recently died, so apparently it was now all right to go there.

Living at Grossmama's turned out to be quite wonderful. There were so many rooms in her apartment to play in and lots of old, comfortable furniture. Both Grossmama and Aunt Gerda were kind and loving. They played games with me, read me stories, and we would talk in funny rhymes to each other. Then there was Pütz, the beautiful German shepherd, who was my special friend, I could hug and play with for hours.

On Sundays there were often excursions by boat to famous landmarks on the Rhine. We visited castles, and even climbed up to the top of the rock where the legendary Lorelei used to sit and comb her long, blond hair while enticing sailors. They who would watch her instead of the dangerous rocks that would ultimately shipwreck them. I really looked forward to these outings, especially since they usually included ice cream in one of the cafes on the mountain top.

Grossmama's cooking was wonderful too. The whole

family sat around the huge dining-room table. My place was next to my great-uncle Eugene. He was always telling jokes that I didn't understand, although they made everyone laugh. I remember he had a special Delft blue plate with margarine, which I was allowed to share with him. To this day, I still prefer the margarine of my youth to real butter.

Sadly, years later, I found out that on the Kristallnacht in 1938, Uncle Eugen was one of the hundreds of Jews who were dragged from their homes by the Nazis, beaten, and left on the street to die.

After a few enjoyable months at Grossmama's, Daddy, on one of his rare visits, said to me, "You're going to be living with me from now on, because your mother doesn't want you anymore."

There it was again. I didn't believe it at first, but when Mutti didn't come to see me even once, I realized that it was true. She had a new baby now, so I thought she probably didn't need me anymore.

My things got packed up, and I was driven to my father's new house in the small town of Krefeld, just seventeen kilometers from Düsseldorf. Such vast difference to the warmth I had just come from. The house had two floors. The downstairs was Daddy's surgery. I was strictly forbidden to go in there, but I was allowed to go through the backdoor to the courtyard to play with Bobby, our boxer. The upstairs had two bedrooms, a combined living and dining room and a big kitchen. I shared one of the bedrooms with Anna, the housekeeper. She was the one who had cooked the fresh asparagus that was to be such a special treat, but instead set the tone for the difficult relationship I would have with my father.

Cookies

My father and my stepmother Alice settled in Amsterdam when I was nine. They had found an apartment a few blocks away from Alice's parents in a predominantly Jewish neighborhood. I had my own room, but the largest room with a bath was rented out to a seamstress. Irma was our maid. She took care of the cooking, the cleaning, and me.

It didn't take me long to learn Dutch, ride a bicycle with ease, or fit into the new country. My father, however, not being a Dutch citizen, was not permitted to practice medicine, so he found a job as a salesman for a pharmaceutical company.

These years in Holland from age nine to fourteen were likely the most normal years of my childhood. Although because of age requirements, I attended several different schools, this was true for other children as well, so I was not such an outsider.

I often had a feeling that if I were a boy, my father might love me, so I excelled at athletics: long jumping and broad jumping were easy with my long legs, but I was also good at discus, javelin throw, and shot put. Like a boy, I also got into all kinds of mischief. I climbed forbidden trees, climbed on top of the synagogue when I was supposed to be in it, and hid the early morning milk deliveries so that people couldn't find them for breakfast.

Even at this early age, I was fascinated by human behavior. My friend Elizabeth and I would attach coins to a long string and drop them in front of passersbyer, and then watch with glee as they scrambled for the coins that we then pulled away.

Sometimes we would stand on the street, look up at nothing, and start laughing hysterically. Pretty soon a crowd of people had stopped and joined the laughter, having no idea what was so funny.

Once I fell into the canal. I was not supposed to walk along the edge on my way to school. Instead of being sympathetic at my being sopping wet and losing my wings, which meant I would have to miss being an angel in the school pageant, I was severely punished.

After school, I was usually eager to share what I had learned that day, so that I consistently forgot to put away the garbage cans before I came upstairs to our apartment. When Alice mentioned this to my father, he reprimanded me and condemned me to his favorite punishment—I was to write five hundred times: "I must not forget to bring in the garbage cans." I felt that punishment to be totally unjust, because as soon as I was reminded, I cheerfully put the cans away.

At the age of twelve, I decided it was time to leave home for good. I unearthed my winter coat, since my plan was to stay away long past the summer, and I crept out of the house. I had successfully escaped, but there was one problem, I didn't have any place to go. I wandered around for a while, finally ending up at a friend's house, but when I heard her mother on the telephone with my father, I got out of there fast. I found myself in a field near home. I found a place to hide in the bushes where I could also sleep, but my father found me (how, I'll never know), grabbed me by the collar, and dragged me home.

"Now sit down and finish your lines." I wrote well into the night.

I tried to be helpful around the house, hoping for my father's approval, but when I couldn't get that, I found all sorts of ways to outsmart him. For instance, I would wet my toothbrush, but not brush my teeth. Then, when he questioned me, my answer was, "Of course I brushed my teeth, Daddy, you can check my toothbrush."

I must have been about twelve when outsmarting my father took a more sophisticated form; it was all about cookies. At night when my parents went to bed, my father would put his change and the huge bunch of keys he carried onto a small metal stand in their bathroom. The door to their bedroom was always left open.

One night I waited until I heard the heavy breathing that indicated my parents were asleep. Then I tiptoed barefoot into the bathroom, quietly closed their bedroom door and turned on the light. Next I studied the exact position of every one of those twenty keys on that metal stand. Without making a sound I picked up the entire bunch and brought them into the living room.

Once I found the key that opened the cupboard where all the goodies were kept, I took the box of cookies and emptied the entire box onto the towel I had spread on the floor. I put the empty box back, relocked the cupboard and took the loot back to my room. Before I tasted even one crumb, I performed the delicate task of returning the keys to that metal stand in exactly the same position as they had been. The money that was there didn't interest me; I was only after the cookies that were always kept locked up. I quietly opened the door to my parents' bedroom and got back to my room without incident. At last, I was able to devour those cookies, and I enjoyed them with an exhilarated sense of triumph. Alice asked me a few days later, "Gisela, did you take cookies from the cupboard in the living room?" With an air of complete innocence, I answered, "I couldn't have taken them. Isn't that cupboard always kept locked, and doesn't Daddy have the only key?"

After a while, the stealing became more sophisticated. Disguised in dark glasses and a babushka, I would place an order at a neighborhood grocery store, to be delivered to a fake name and address, saying to the clerk, "My mother got unexpected company and she needs the cookies right away. Could I please take them with me?"

"Of course, dear."

Eventually I would ride my bike to grocery stores all over Amsterdam and pull the same stunt. It worked every time. Once, when a girl called me a dirty Jew in the school yard, I had a large order delivered to her house, minus the cookies. I was delighted when she was punished.

I kept my cookies hidden in a space I had dug in a nearby field. Some boards across the top, covered with clumps of grass, made a wonderful hiding place. This way I had an endless supply of cookies. I never had to ask for any, and so I never ran the risk of being refused.

Enemy Alien

In 1938, five years after we had settled in Amsterdam, the Nazis threatened to invade Holland. My father had made contact with some distant cousins in Cleveland, Ohio, and they had agreed to sponsor him in the United States. So, just before Holland was invaded, my family escaped the Nazis a second time, and made their way to the United States.

At the time, plans were uncertain for my father and Alice, so, I was sent on my own to Bournemouth, a resort town on the south coast of England. It was here that my father's younger sister Gerda, after emigrating from Hitler's Germany, had established a new home and a dental practice.

I said goodbye to my friend Elizabeth upstairs and gave a tearful hug to Lotto, my furry best friend downstairs. I was taken to Ostend, and from there to Dover on the ferry, then to Bournemouth by train. It was only an overnight boat trip, but the waters of the English Channel are notoriously rough, and they made me deathly seasick.

Jeannette Cohen, the wife of a cousin of ours, was instrumental in placing Jewish refugee children. I was sent to

Leeson House, a boarding school for girls, right across the bay from Bournemouth, and accessible only by ferry boat.

There were twenty-four girls in the school. I was put in the lowest grade—a class of six-year-olds, although I was fourteen, because the only English I knew was "yes," "no," "I don't know," and "God Save the King." The year of French I had in Holland enabled me to communicate with the French teacher at least until I learned English. After three months, I spoke pretty fluently and successfully moved up through the grades. I did submit an essay on "How George Bernard Shaw Betrayed Joan of Arc," when the assignment had been how he had "portrayed" her. Well, it sounded like "betrayed" to me, so that's what I wrote. The girls in my class had a good laugh at that, but the teacher definitely did not.

Along with the other Jewish girl who had been placed in my school, I was made to feel inferior. Our school uniforms were even made of cheaper material, so that when the other girls looked crisp and fresh, we always looked wrinkled. It was around this time I became very self-conscious about my appearance. We were considered charity cases and were not allowed to participate in theater trips or any special outings. Instead, we were given extra homework or sometimes sewing assignments. I had a great desire to play the piano, but any extras such as music or painting had a charge and were off limits to us.

I also found it difficult that the British stiff upper lip frowned upon any show of my emotion. When I received letters, I was severely reprimanded for my excitement—jumping up and down was not allowed. During these two years, I continued to withdraw further into myself, feeling fewer emotions.

Holidays I spent with my aunt Gerda, then with Gerda and Grossmama, once Grossmama came to live with her. My aunts had finally convinced Grossmama that she might be killed like her brother Eugen during Kristallnacht if she stayed in Düsseldorf any longer. The innocuous name Selo and her kind landlady could not protect her much longer.

Gerda gave up her bedroom to her mother and slept on the daybed in the living room. I slept downstairs in the waiting room of her surgery, which had a separate street entrance, then came upstairs to warm up and have breakfast.

In pre–World War II Britain, life could often seem primitive. For example, there was no central heating. A small gas heater had to suffice in Gerda's apartment on Richmond Hill to keep us warm in the damp English weather. In order to take a bath, the water heater needed to be turned on at least an hour ahead of time. With three of us needing to bathe, this was quite time consuming. To speed things along, I would often wash using the kitchen sink, while Gerda was taking her lengthy once-a-week bath.

Marga, my other aunt, although trained as a social worker, found a job as housekeeper in a huge house owned by a British spinster, Miss Payne. Provided I did not disturb her, Marga allowed me to stay with her on some holidays. On these privileged occasions, I was on my best behavior.

Life was terribly strict for my willful teenage self. I was not allowed to go to the cinema by myself, but I was desperate to see films since I had only seen Shirley Temple movies, and once The Four Feathers, while at school. But while at Miss Payne's, Aunt Marga had no say over my activities. So, one morning I said to Miss Payne, "A funny film, *Mr. Doodle Kicks*

Off, is playing at the cinema. Do you think I could go to see it this afternoon?"

Since Miss Payne didn't quite know what to do with a teenager all day long, she gave me permission. I neglected to tell her that *Mr. Doodle Kicks Off* was part of a double feature with the film *Love Affair*. When I arrived at the cinema, I skipped Mr. Doodle and totally lost myself in *Love Affair*, featuring Charles Boyer and Irene Dunne. To this day it's one of my favorite movies. Such a wonderful romantic story! I wanted so much to be loved. This movie confirmed to my young heart that love was out there.

In 1939, Oma and Opa Keyzer, my stepmother Alice's parents, invited me to Amsterdam for my summer vacation. When I arrived, Oma looked at my pigtails and round face and immediately took me to have my hair cut. My pigtails gave me the appearance of a "Hitlermädchen," a "Hitler youth." Oma's next step was to have me fitted for a bra. I was so grateful to now feel like young lady rather than a child. Other than the bra, it was not much fun staying with the Keyzers. Oma had a cold and forbidding demeanor and always made me feel uncomfortable. By this time, my friend Gabi had already emigrated to the United States with her family, and Anne Frank had disappeared. I had no friends. There were endless boring visits to cousins I had never met before, all on Alice's side of the family, and of no blood relation to me.

One day during my vacation, Opa sat me down and told me it was possible that England would shortly declare war on Germany, and civilians would no longer be allowed to cross the English Channel. I understood that if I stayed, I would have to remain in Holland with them until the war ended. Knowing this, I chose to end my vacation early and return to England. Opa congratulated me on my intelligent choice.

It was an adventurous trip back, I flirted outrageously with a number of men on the ship, and 'lo and behold, just after I had fallen asleep, somebody woke me up in my cabin with some very pleasant but unexpected caresses. It was the ship's handsome purser! Fortunately for me, he discovered that I was wearing a sanitary belt (we didn't have tampons in those days), and he gently left my cabin. For a long time, I worried that his passionate kisses had gotten me pregnant, for Alice had told me some such story once. When I was finally sure I was not, in fact, pregnant, I realized how traveling as a lone and innocent teen could have had very serious consequences.

On August 29, 1939, I arrived back in England. War broke out on September 3. If I had not returned to England, I would have perished along with Oma and Opa Keyzer and all my cousins still in Amsterdam. Not one of them survived. I missed this fate by a mere five days—I was safely back in Bournemouth.

In 1940, it seemed certain that Germany would attempt to invade England. Winston Churchill passed a law requiring all enemy aliens (I still had a German passport) to move at least five miles away from the coast. Bournemouth was a seaside resort, right on the ocean, so we were forced to move.

Grossmama and both my aunts were relocated to Cheltenham, near Gloucester, England. I was sent to an isolated farm near the Welsh border. Inexperienced with the English language, I couldn't understand a word Mr. and Mrs. Organ said, their dialect was so different. In addition, life here was primitive. The many luxuries city girls take for granted were gone: electricity, indoor toilets, even running water. Mrs. Organ used to wash my hair outside, pumping cold water from the well. Each day I was expected to walk miles over the hills to attend the country school and to church on Sundays. Completely out of place in these surroundings, I hardly spoke to anyone. I just felt numb and detached the entire time I was there.

During my time with The Organs, my father was busy in the United States where he completed his internship at Mt. Sinai Hospital in Cleveland, Ohio. Unlike most of his colleagues, he had passed the Ohio State Board on his very first try. With his new license in the United States, he opened a medical practice in Findlay, a small, wealthy, and waspish town in northern Ohio. Rather than be lumped together with the multitude of other Jewish refugees in the big city, my father assumed he would achieve greater success in the small town of Findlay.

Findlay, Ohio

By the summer of 1940, Britain had descended fully into the conflict with Germany. Every day, the reality of wartime terror cast its shadow over us, as German planes bombarded the country with bombs. After only a few weeks on the Organ family farm, I was taken to Liverpool. Here, I joined a small group of other children awaiting a ship to the United States. It was a frightening time—Having turned in our gas masks, we spent every night scared this would be the night the Germans would choose to attack with gas weapon, rather than regular bombs.

At last the day came when the *Duchess of Athol*, a Canadian ship, arrived and we began our journey across the ocean to Toronto, Canada. For several weeks, we were packed together below deck, while our ship evaded the threat of German submarines. I remember little else from the passage across the Atlantic. When we finally arrived in Toronto, we were swiftly herded into several hotel rooms—I was kept locked alone in a room all night long. It was my father's second wife, my stepmother Alice, who showed up the next day to claim me, and drive me to their new home in Findlay, Ohio. I was just sixteen when I arrived in this foreign little town.

With a population of 25,000 people and only ten Jewish families, my father, Alice and I stood out in Findlay. As the first refugee family here, the local paper even included a feature on us that included photographs. I did not appreciate the added attention and I grew more self-conscious. To make matters worse, my clothes trunk was delayed several weeks. My photo debut could not have been more humiliating—I had no choice but to stuff my size fourteen body into one of Alice's much too small housedresses.

I entered the local high school, Findlay High School, as part of the junior class. As soon as the novelty of "refugee" wore off, I was treated like an intruder. With my British accent I was perceived as "stuck up" in the Midwest and turned the other kids off. I was so different from the girls my age in high school. In Europe at sixteen, I was still considered a child, guarded and sheltered from the adolescent life of America. I was totally ignorant about teenagers' favorite topics of conversation: boys, movies and movie stars, and football and basketball. I knew nothing of the musical favorites of the day: Bing Crosby, Glenn Miller, and Harry James. Dancing, especially the jitterbug, was something I didn't even dare to attempt, and I had never been out on a date. I owned no saddle shoes, wore no make-up, and when I tried to chew gum, it fell out of my mouth. To make matters worse, I was ahead academically, and although I was proud of being the only junior in the senior math class, it didn't exactly endear me to the other kids. I was never invited to a party or asked on a date, and I ended up feeling like even more of an outsider than I had in England. More than ever I needed moral support at home, but instead I received the full brunt of my father's disappointment. I always felt that I was in the way.

Because I was tall, could jump, and was good at basketball, I was elected as president of the GAA (Girls Athletic Association) in my senior year at Findlay High. Instead of being supportive, my father accused me of always pushing myself into the limelight. He never once attended a game. His reaction was similar when I was cast as a main character in the senior play. He was never proud, only disappointed. Even my grades, mostly As, weren't good enough. I could do nothing right, and anytime I felt a sense of accomplishment, he was completely disinterested. I was worthless in his eyes. There was no way to please this man. His stinging words, "There was peace in this house until the day you arrived," still echo in my ears. It seemed clear to me—my father would have preferred if I had stayed in England and been killed by a German bomb. This new life was miserable and lonely.

I made a single friend, Doris, truly one of the nicest girls in my class. Although I enjoyed attending many of her family dinners, I was never allowed to return the invitation. Doris came from the wrong side of the tracks, and my father and Alice made it known that she was not welcome at our house.

I was eighteen when one of the local college students invited me out on my very first date. The boy came to pick me up and politely greeted my father, who proceeded to give him the third degree about his background and his future intentions toward me. He made him promise to have me home by 9:30 p.m., which meant that we had to leave the movie before it was over. I never heard from that boy again. That was the only date I had until I arrived at college. I couldn't wait to leave home, and so

I started at the University of Michigan in the summer term of 1942, right after graduating from Findlay High.

Alice

My stepmother Alice was just nineteen when she married my father back in Germany on August 6, 1930. Until they married, she had led an incredibly privileged and sheltered life, free of responsibility. Now, she was expected to deal with a troubled six-year-old. I say "troubled" because my father had just told me that my Mutti didn't want me anymore. It was all terribly confusing to my six-year-old developing brain. I had many questions but I dared not burden my father and his young bride. Now—I thought at the time—I have a new Mutti.

This new mummy was very pretty, slender, and fashionable. She had no idea what to do with me, and alas, she never would. Sadly, it was so simple: I needed to feel loved, but I don't think Alice was capable of love. Throughout the many years we knew each other, she was never affectionate with me. I believe we were both at fault when it came to the emotional distance between us, and partly due to her own personality.

When I was six and they were first married, they took me along on a vacation to a resort in Austria. I remember many details from that trip because it was the only time in fifteen years that they ever took me along.

I experienced subtle, but constant put-downs from Alice. They may not have been intentional, but they caused me to feel deeply insecure. To this day, I struggle to about what to wear and how to behave in various social situations. She would buy me clothes as if she were purchasing something for herself— they never flattered my curvier figure or my coloring. Sweaters hugged my ample bosom too tightly, and I began to slouch out of self-consciousness. Alice used to say her chest was as flat as two fried eggs; I guess that's why she never realized it was about time I start wearing a bra. It was her mother, Omi Keyzer, who finally took me for my first bra, but two years after I was fully developed. When I was seventeen, Alice bought me an expensive mustard-colored herringbone tweed suit. It had only one button, so my chest always popped out in a horribly embarrassing way. Despite my discomfort, I was mannerly, and knew I should grateful, so I kept my lips sealed, smiled, and wore that hideous suit.

Before the senior prom Alice took me to Patterson's, the department store in Findlay where she did most of her shopping. The sales ladies greeted her with the familiarity of an old friend. In the dress department, I was fitted with an olive-green velvet dress. Our next stop was the hosiery department. Alice explained, "Ruthie (as I was known then) needs stockings to go with her new prom dress, but not too sheer." A proper pair was chosen and neatly wrapped in a parcel. As we were leaving, Alice pivoted back to face the sales lady, "I need some new stockings for everyday wear. Please, just add three pairs in my size to the order." I was mortified.

Just before I my departure for college, I asked if I could go shopping by myself. I was given fifteen dollars, presumably for one new summer dress. Instead of buying one dress, I found a shop on the "wrong side of the tracks" and returned with three, five-dollar dresses. They were the favorite part of my wardrobe all through college.

I suspect Alice had great influence over my father's opinion of me at other times too. Once, I overheard Alice talking to my father, ridiculing my boyfriend, Mike, and me, as we walked arm in arm.

Over the years Alice sent me a variety of gifts. One was a fancy box of soaps out of which she had forgotten to take the card that read: "To Alice from Cele." One year I got one of those heavy Norwegian ski sweaters; how come Alice, always so fashion-conscious, did not realize that I did not need reindeer running across my bosom. Those are some of my early memories of Alice.

After my father's death, Alice remarried, and she and her new husband, Henry Herman, bought a lovely house in Armonk, an upscale suburb of New York. To me, she seemed like a luxury plant that had simply been transplanted into a new pot. During the ten years I was a soprano soloist at the Episcopal Church in nearby Rye, New York, I would regularly call Alice. Some Sundays I was invited to lunch between my rehearsal and church service. After a very formal lunch on the patio, Henry would retire, and I would help Alice in the kitchen while we talked about whatever was happening in my life. It felt important to maintain contact with her.

Later in life, cold, snowy winters prompted Alice and Henry to move south to Palm Beach, Florida, and slowly their health declined. Henry had diabetes and one of his legs was amputated. Alice had glaucoma and was gradually losing her eyesight. John, the son of Henry's long-time friend, regularly travelled to Palm Beach to assist them. I called as often as I could, but I was glad they had his help, for I had little money and was not familiar with their affairs. After Henry passed away, John made all the funeral arrangements and took care of Henry's estate. He continued to visit Alice every couple of weeks, pampering her with flowers and outings, while also looking after her finances. Once, I offered to drive down for a visit, but her answer was, "Well, I can't sit and talk for long periods anymore." I got the message—she wasn't interested in seeing me. Still, out of some deep-rooted sense of loyalty and concern, I continued to call her at least once every two weeks.

As Alice's faculties declined, the prime and proper demeanor I knew so well faded, and I realized how little she cared about me. Once, when she returned one of my calls, my answering machine—with a greeting by an automated male voice—took her message: "Hello, are you this lady's husband? Please tell her that Alice called."

I had been divorced for over ten years and Alice no idea. She had never listened to me over all the years I kept in touch. For a long time, I saved that message on my machine—It was evidence of her apathy towards me, even though I was the only person to ever call her Mummy. She never had children of her own.

Years later I located my birth mother and two half-siblings, I called Alice to tell her that I was going to visit my brother in Düsseldorf. He was terminally ill with cancer, and I wanted to get to know him before he died. Alice then told me how difficult it had been to adopt John, because his mother was still alive in Hungary. The procedure had taken a very long time, but at last she had succeeded in adopting John. I said, "That's wonderful for you!" And added jokingly: "Now I have another brother!"

"You were never my daughter."

Those words sliced through me like a knife, but they were true. Only in retrospect do I realize my denial.

First Love

As a freshman at the University of Michigan, Ann Arbor, I was thrilled to be asked out on my very first date by Mike Sterngold, a senior engineering student. He was not much taller than I, and slightly overweight. He also wasn't terribly exciting, but he gave me his fraternity pin and told me he loved me. Love-starved as I was, I thought this love was the answer to all my problems. By the end of that first semester, we had plans to marry after his graduation.

I also spent more time in the infirmary than I did in class that first semester. I had been quarantined due to a recurring throat and nasal infection. The dean of women informed me that I would have to undergo a physical before I would be allowed to return to college. I went home to Findlay, and my father took me to a new doctor. Apparently the first ENT specialist had botched my tonsillectomy and my soft palate had collapsed. Under this new doctor, I underwent more operations, including some plastic surgery to raise my soft palate. Then, further complications with this repair surgery: the newly grafted tissue did not heal properly. Air pockets developed between the layers of grafted tissue and filled with infection to form multiple Quinsy abscesses in my mouth. The abscesses recurred over many years, and each one required surgery under general anesthesia. Only a renowned throat specialist at Lenox Hill Hospital was able to eradicate the infection when I was twenty-eight years old.

As I recuperated over the semester break, Mike came to visit me in Findlay, where he also met my father for the first time. His visit was not received well by my father, who threatened to have Mike arrested if he ever came near me again.

Mike and I exchanged daily love letters during this time. I discovered later that my father had opened and read each of these letters. I couldn't wait to get back to Ann Arbor to see Mike. So, although I was still healing, and on a liquid diet, I convinced my parents that I was well enough to go back to school early and take the required physical. No surprise that in my weakened condition I failed the physical. My academic aspirations and Mike would have to wait until the following semester. Heartbroken at the thought of being away from Mike for a whole three months, I made up my mind to leave Findlay and move to Detroit, where I thought I could find a job and see Mike when he came home on weekends. It seemed I had it all figured out—as soon as Mike had his degree, we would get married and live happily ever after. I called home to inform my parents of my plans.

Alice convinced me to come home to recuperate first and then decide what to do. Weak, tired and stressed, she talked me into this plan, a huge mistake.

In those days the trip from Ann Arbor to Findlay involved taking three buses, the last of which stopped in every little village along the way. By the time my father picked me up at the bus depot, it was one o'clock in the morning; I was near collapse. My father took no notice. Once home, he stood me up against the wall and delivered an endless tirade about my character. He wrongly assumed that my dismissal from the university was due to promiscuous relations with Mike and constant tardiness. I was still a virgin. It was true that I had been late once by fifteen minutes when I couldn't pull myself away from *Wuthering Heights* before it ended. No matter, my father ranted and raged; accusing me of being "just like my mother" and at last delivering these devastating words, "You're probably pregnant right now."

I was just leaning against the wall, detached and letting his accusations roll off my back, sorry I had ever returned home. His words were clear, "If I ever catch Mike anywhere near you, I will have him arrested for "delinquency to a minor."

Although I didn't know exactly what this meant, I knew it was a threat against Mike. When I was finally allowed up to my room, I heard the key turn in the lock behind me. I was eighteen years old, locked in my room in my father's house. In the morning, I was let out of my room and my father offered me two choices: "If you really want to go to work, the Cone girls in Cleveland will gladly put you up and will find you an appropriate job." He lit a cigarette and continued, "If you want to finish your studies, Dwight Murray has been kind enough to get permission for you to enroll at Bluffton College. As an alumnus he can get you in without difficulty."

Well, any college sounded better than the four old-maid Cone cousins in Cleveland. So, after some negotiations over the phone, Dwight came to the house to drive me the twenty-five miles to Bluffton. Before I got into the car, my father's last move was to search my pocketbook. Anticipating his actions, I had stowed my letter to Mike in my shoe; once again I had outsmarted him.

Bluffton was a tiny town, it consisted of two blocks on Main Street, a few side streets, and the small college of three hundred students. Near the college, I found a mailbox and sent my letter off to Mike; I wanted him to know what was happening. Oh, how I missed Mike's love and affection.

When I arrived at the dorm, I was given a room on the ground floor. My roommate was Anne, a senior, assigned to keep a watchful eye over me. Anne seemed very nice, and after several days I confided in her, revealing my sad, romantic tale of love and separation. She agreed to help me. Since my mail was being censored, Mike would address his letters to Anne. He would use brown ink, so we would know which letters were for me. Our letters were deeply passionate proclamations of our love, but our actual relationship was quite tame. They say that absence makes the heart grow fonder; indeed, after a six-week separation, we had convinced ourselves we were more passionately in love than ever. We were desperate to be together.

As difficult as it was, we managed to meet early one Sunday morning while everyone from my small Mennonite college was attending church services, Mike and I reunited in an out-of-the-way field. Lying on an old towel, we planned our elopement, interspersed with lots of hugging and kissing.

The Elopement

I was being carefully watched, and I remembered my father's threat to send Mike to jail for "delinquency to a minor." Under these circumstances, Mike and I concluded that our only way to be together was to marry. In 1942, it was out of the question for a couple to live outside the sanctity of marriage. So, we decided to elope.

After some research, Mike discovered that all states required boys under twenty-one to receive parental permission to marry; Mike was sure that he could get that from his father. In Ohio and Michigan, girls under twenty-one were considered minors, which meant I would also need parental consent to marry, which of course I couldn't get. The closest big city where girls were not considered minors at eighteen was Fort Wayne, Indiana, so that's where we had to go, but two more obstacles stood in our way. First, at that time the "Mann Act" made transporting a minor over the state line a crime punishable with jail time. This worried Mike. To evade this law, he told me to borrow enough money to prove that I was able to pay for the trip across the state line myself. Second, we needed to time the escape so as not be seen by my chaperone. We pinpointed the perfect time. Two afternoons a week, I walked twenty minutes from the college to Main Street for a babysitting job. The job was easy—I watched two kids, fed them, helped them with their homework, and put them to bed. It was these twenty minutes that gave me a certain freedom. The mother was usually home by 9:30 p.m., and I was expected back in the dorm by 10:00 p.m.

Mike checked out the bus schedules and lined up what we'd need for our blood tests and marriage license. Then we set our date: Sunday, November 1, 1942.

The night before our flight, I asked several girls in the dorm to lend me some money, and thus I managed to get together twenty dollars to cross the state line. On Sunday morning, while everyone was in church, I packed a small bag and hid it in the bushes behind the dormitory. After babysitting that evening, I planned to pick up my bag, and immediately board the nine o'clock bus to Lima. Mike would set out from Detroit, make the necessary connections, and meet me on that same bus.

Before we even set out that evening there was a hitch. One of the dorm girls had overheard my attempts to borrow money and had reported this to the headmistress, Miss Anderson. As I was leaving the building to go to my job that Sunday afternoon, Miss Anderson called me into her office. "Gisela, why do you need extra money?"

Totally unprepared to answer her question, I decided to tell her everything. I revealed that Mike and I were to meet on the bus, that we would stop in Lima for the night, then take the 5:00 a.m. bus to Fort Wayne. She listened with interest, then, almost regretfully, sighed. "Gisela, you realize that it is my duty as headmistress to inform your father of your intention to run off and get married."

I pleaded with her to at least wait until the next morning before calling my father to inform him and finally she relented. Much relieved, I proceeded as planned. I retrieved my bag from the bushes and walked to my babysitting job on Main Street. The children's mother promised to be back by 8:30 p.m. Perfect. As soon as she left, I called the college and told them the mother had to work overtime and had asked me to spend the night. This would account for my absence from the college later that evening.

At 8:30 p.m., the mother returned home, and I let her know I was leaving Bluffton for good that night. I hugged the kids goodbye, grabbed my suitcase, and went downstairs to wait for the bus. As I waited, I felt excited and nervous about our plan. A candy store on Main Street served as the bus depot and was in plain sight, but luckily, construction had rerouted the bus to a side street, so I could be more discrete. But there was still the fact that Mike had to travel from Detroit to Toledo and from there catch the connecting bus to Lima. The Lima bus stopped in Bluffton by special request.

Finally, the bus arrived. I looked through the window for Mike but didn't see him. Oh God, what if Mike wasn't on the bus? What on earth would I do then? It was too late for me to go back to the dorm, so I boarded the bus. The bus driver took my fare and then, with a big grin, motioned with his head toward the back of the bus. There was Mike, crouched on the floor between the seats, making sure that he couldn't be seen from the street. He had told the driver his story, and that dear man had agreed to say his only passenger was a young lady who got on in Bluffton. He wouldn't even let Mike pay, so there would be no record of his being on the bus.

We arrived in Fort Wayne, more relaxed now that we were together. After thanking the driver profusely, we found a small hotel near the bus depot. It had to be inexpensive, between the two of us we only had but thirty-five dollars. I was bursting with excitement as we registered as Mr. and Mrs., but Mike was so nervous, he could barely sign the register. Alone in our room at last, we hugged and kissed, but when the time came to undress, we were both shy. I went into the bathroom and put on my pajamas. Then it was Mike's turn, and he dawdled as much as I had. In spite of what my father thought, we were both completely inexperienced. When we finally got into bed, well after midnight, we tried to make love, but it just didn't work. After much awkward fumbling, we finally fell asleep in each other's arms. It was as I had dreamed—someone to hold and someone to love. Exactly what I thought marriage was all about.

When the alarm went off at 4:00 a.m., we couldn't break from each other's arms; we reset the alarm for 6:00 a.m. We were even too late to make the 7:00 a.m. bus. Instead, we went for coffee and arrived with plenty of time for the 9:00 a.m. bus to Fort Wayne.

We had planned to get everything done in one day, and as soon as we arrived in Fort Wayne that Monday morning, November 2, we found a lab for our blood tests. We were slightly delayed when Mike passed out while his blood was being drawn, but no matter, the lab promised that the tests would be ready later that afternoon. Next, we walked to the courthouse for our marriage license. With no waiting period in Indiana, we got our license right away. It was 4:30 p.m. by the time we received test results from the lab. We ran back to the courthouse, but the Justice of the Peace had left for the day. We would have to wait one more day.

Hungry, with barely enough money to cover another night's lodging, we spotted a place where twenty-five cents bought a plate of spaghetti with bread. We lingered over the meal; after all, this was our wedding dinner! Afterward, we found a hotel charging fifty cents a bed. And a bed was all we got. There was a bathroom down the hall, but no toilet paper or running water. We told ourselves that by tomorrow we would be married and everything would be fine, but at 2:00 a.m. things took another turn for the worse when Mike developed a raging toothache! I tried to make him a compress, but with no running water, our second night together turned into a nightmare.

Toothache or not, the next morning we headed to the courthouse to legalize our now illicit affair! Imagine our dismay when we were informed that the courthouse was closed; it was the first Tuesday in November, Election Day. There was no one to marry us. We were devastated. With only enough money to pay the Justice of the Peace plus our bus fare back to Detroit, I broke down. A sympathetic clerk at the information window, seeing me in tears, offered to help. After a quick phone call, she informed us she that she had found someone who would marry us that same day. Following her directions, we soon found ourselves in front of a minister's house.

After all the chaos, everything was finally in place: we had the license, the minister to marry us, and his wife and daughter to be our witnesses. The Protestant ceremony was totally unfamiliar to both of us, as Mike was also Jewish. During the service, the minister said, "In the name of the Father, the Son, and the Holy Ghost." In response, Mike immediately shouted "Harry!" Although the minister didn't understand, I realized right away that Mike thought he was being asked for his father's name; I began to giggle, rather hysterically. The minister set out to say a few words about the meaning of marriage, but Mike cut him short. "What do we owe you?"

Somewhat taken aback, the minister said, "Well, whatever you care to give."

Mike pressed our last two dollars into his hand, and we reached for our coats. The family must have thought us totally insane, but we walked happily away, arm in arm to the bus station. Now we were Mr. and Mrs. Milton Leon Sterngold!

Neither Mike nor his father had said anything about our marriage to Mrs. Sterngold. When we arrived unexpectedly at his mother's apartment in Detroit, she wasn't too pleased. With reluctance, she allowed us to sleep on the Murphy bed in her living room until we found a place of our own. Not much of a honeymoon, but we were together. The stress of Fort Wayne behind us, we were content to simply be together.

In Detroit, I wrote my father a long letter. I explained that I had to be with Mike; he was the only person in the world who made me feel wanted and loved. I had eloped for love, not as an act of rebellion to spite him.

A week or so later, I took the bus back to Bluffton College to retrieve the rest of my belongings. Before leaving, I went to Miss Anderson to thank her. Puzzled she said, "But I didn't wait! After you left, I consulted my minister. He convinced me that my duty and responsibility as headmistress took precedence over my promise to you, and so I informed your father that same evening." Then coldly she added, "Apparently everything you told me was a lie. Your father drove over from Findlay that evening and waited for the bus from Toledo, but there was no bus."

I imagined my father sitting in his car on Main Street, waiting to catch me with Mike. He had no idea the bus was rerouted to a side street. Miss Anderson continued, "Your father then drove on to Lima hoping to catch up with you there. The bus had already arrived. When he questioned the bus driver, the driver told him that he only had one passenger, a young girl getting on at Bluffton. Your father searched all of Lima for a young girl rather than a couple." She paused before finishing. "He then figured that you had lied to me, but just in case, waited at the bus depot for the 5:00 a.m. and even the 7:00 a.m. bus to Fort Wayne, but there was no sign of you. Then he concluded he should have known better than to believe anything you told me since, after all, you were a pathological liar just like your mother. Frustrated, furious, and totally exhausted, he gave up and drove back to Findlay."

When I realized that my father had been right behind us that whole night, but didn't catch us, I felt that old sense of triumph once again at having outsmarted him. But any feeling of satisfaction was destroyed by his letter to me in answer to my letter of explanation, which ended with the words: "I could have the marriage annulled, but you're not worth the trouble."

Divorce

In Detroit, Mike and I found a dingy two-room apartment, furnishings included. It seemed like heaven to me: I easily got a job at a dress shop, selling dresses and designing the window displays. I can't recall what odd job Mike found; we were together for only two months when he was drafted into the Army. I was devastated. Marital bliss soon turned to being alone in an empty apartment.

Mike left for basic training in New Jersey. I quickly followed him to the East Coast. In Teaneck, he found me a room with another service member's wife and their small baby. To support myself, I first got a job printing signs in a Jersey City department store. After a few weeks I was promoted to the dress department as a salesclerk. I saved on food because I could eat on the base in the mess hall, and then take the bus home.

At first, I managed quite well, until one day I caught a bad cold. That night I returned home to my Teaneck lodging and my landlady refused to let me in the house, fearing the baby would catch my illness. I took the bus back to Jersey City and sat on a bench somewhere. I didn't know where to go. I was feverish and coughing. Somehow, I managed to find my way to a Red Cross office where I passed out. The Red Cross tried to contact my husband, but he had been transferred to Watertown, New York, and was in quarantine. The next thing I knew, I was being fed chicken soup by an elderly lady. She had taken me in, and soon nursed me back to health. She even gave me money to retrieve my things from Teaneck.

I took a bus to Watertown, where I answered an advertisement for a live-in maid in a boarding house. I made beds, cleaned the bathrooms, and waited on tables. In between these chores, I peeled potatoes and onions and hulled peas. I was able to see Mike only rarely, but at least I knew he was close by.

Mike received a medical discharge, based on asthma and hay fever and we returned to Michigan. In Michigan, we found a lovely apartment in the house of my sociology professor, Dr. Newcombe. By this time, the initial thrill of marriage had worn off—there was no "separation to make the heart grow fonder." I began to see Mike for who he was. He could not keep up with me physically or mentally. While I moved swiftly with my long legs, he lingered half a block behind. I could see myself dragging him along for the rest of my life, and I was only nineteen.

We both found jobs in a cafeteria on campus, but Mike lasted only a week. He was too slow and inefficient. I carried a full credit load of classes, kept house, did the laundry, and worked. My grades were excellent, whereas Mike flunked several of his courses. He blamed everything on his being Jewish instead of taking responsibility for himself. I lost all respect for him, and no longer felt sexually attracted to him. After just two years of marriage, I filed for a legal separation. After three years, I was free of him.

My father had been paying my college tuition, but I had to earn all my other expenses. Now divorced, I was considered a fallen woman. There was fear that I would taint the innocence of my dormmates, and I was barred from living in the dorm. As an alternative, I found a rooming house near campus, where I met several handsome South American medical students. This marked my start on the road to sexual freedom. That last year at Michigan marked many changes in my life. I went pretty wild. I kept a list of the men I went to sleep with—they were mostly one-night stands. When I reached one hundred, I decided to stop counting. Strangely enough, if I really liked someone, I wouldn't go to bed with him, insisting we remain friends.

I was introduced to Elsa Minor, a girl from an upstate farm, and we found a two-room apartment right on State Street, just one block from the university. We shared the bathroom and the kitchen with the other apartments on our floor. I would eat breakfast every morning at the drugstore right across the street, but the rest of my meals were free at the cafeteria where I worked.

Our greatest pleasure was lying in the sun on a little patch of flat roof just outside our apartment. We felt carefree. When we went out to sunbathe, we didn't bother to lock our doors. We thought nothing of leaving our jewelry and purses on our beds. One day things began missing from our apartment. At first it was Elsa's cigarette case and my gold necklace. Then money started disappearing from our purses. One day, I noticed Mike on the street near my apartment. What was he doing in my neighborhood? I became suspicious and taking a stab in the dark, I confronted him, "Why did you want to see me?"

Mike made some lame excuse about papers, but instinct

told me Mike had been coming into the apartment and taking our valuables. I decided to visit Mike's girlfriend and warn her. As soon as I mentioned the stolen items, she excused herself for a minute and returned with my necklace and Elsa's cigarette case.

"Are these the things you were talking about?"

I nodded. She handed the items back to me, and then burst into tears. Later on, she married him anyway. Maybe she looked up to him and that was what he needed—something I couldn't do. Our divorce was probably as beneficial for Mike as it was for me.

My Mother

One Sunday, my father asked me to lunch at a fancy hotel in Toledo, the halfway point between Findlay and Ann Arbor. This was an unusual invitation—I was never included in my father's plans. The meal was uneventful, but after finishing, my father led me to the lobby to have a chat. He spoke in a detached manner, as if reading from one of his patients' charts, "Your mother was an extremely unstable woman and created nothing but problems. After a suicide attempt, she was committed to a mental institution for several months. The doctors said she was a pathological liar with a hysterical personality." He lit a cigarette and continued. "She was reckless with my money and spent extravagantly. We were plagued by debt. Every penny I earned, she spent without a second thought. When you were only a few months old, she went on a shopping spree. Then she ran off with you to Baden-Baden, the lavish and costly German spa, for two weeks! Your mother was completely out of control."

I listened to my father in stoic silence. Lighting another cigarette, he went on. "Your mother's spending left us destitute, and the court considered her the "guilty party" in our divorce. I was given sole custody of you. In spite of this, I was generous—I let her raise you for several years. But, as soon as my financial circumstances improved, I removed you from her unstable environment. A few years after our divorce, your mother denounced me to the Nazis—I was warned that my arrest was imminent, and compelled to leave everything behind and flee Germany in the middle of the night."

My father didn't wait a moment for a response. Instead, he looked down at his watch. "Well, I must get back to Findlay—I have a patient this afternoon." With a peck on the cheek he was gone.

I was left stunned and alone in the lobby. According to my father, my mother, had abandoned me at the age of five. But it was my father and his family who had severed ties completely with my mother. I had no idea what she looked like—my father had taken a pair of scissors and removed her face from each and every photograph. Many years later while clearing out the attic after my father's death, I found several letters that shed more light on my father's rejection. The letters were from his mother and sister. They were hateful letters, denouncing me with phrases such as "never mind Gisela, after all, she's just like her mother."

Rock Bottom

It was the fall of 1953, my roommate Evelyn and I let a woman by the name of Marie stay on our couch until she found an apartment of her own. Marie had returned to New York after spending the summer on Cape Cod trying to paint.

One day, the three of us went down to Greenwich Village. We stopped at a restaurant for a bite and ran into one of Marie's acquaintances from Cape Cod. His name was Eliseo Del Rio. He was dark and handsome, of Spanish heritage, and a struggling artist. I was immediately attracted to his intensely good looks and his charisma. Del Rio was a storyteller. He told us he had fought against Franco in the Spanish Civil War and had a metal plate in his head as a result of his wounds. Later on, I learned that he indeed had a metal plate in his head, but because at fifteen he had landed on a rusty nail. However, it was true that he had fought in the Spanish Civil War and was a dedicated communist. All through Greenwich Village, he was known as Del Rio, but I called him just plain Del.

Shortly after we met, Del invited me out to a movie. In retrospect, I should have realized then and there that he had emotional problems—on our first date, he cursed out the cabdriver for getting stuck in traffic, then got out of the cab and walked away without paying. But those piercing black eyes of his had an effect on me. The attraction between us was intense. When he revealed that he had been diagnosed with paranoid schizophrenia, this in no way diminished the attraction. In fact, I wonder if it didn't add to my infatuation.

I was at a low point in my life. My very first psychotherapist had been drafted and left New York City. By the time I met Del, I was plagued by deep feelings of abandonment and loneliness. Del was talented in many ways: he could build things and he enjoyed cooking for me. He also loved music and would sing Spanish songs while playing his guitar. He was an incredibly talented painter. A true artist. Del also wrote wild poetry about the Elysian Fields (because his name was Eliseo, he identified with those Elysian Fields). A deep thinker, he was much preoccupied with the philosophies related to death and religion. I had never met anyone like him. He lived as a "starving artist" washing dishes or waiting on tables, earning free meals and a place to show his paintings that occasionally sold.

Del and I had been going together for several months, when I missed my period. When I missed it a second month, I went to see my gynecologist. After I told him the reason for my visit, he instructed me to return around 6:00 p.m. when he would be alone, the office emptied.

I arrived on time and he spoke freely to me. In my desperation, I was misled to believe I had one option: I could have a series of three injections over a number of weeks that would take care of any pregnancy. The choice was clear, and

I received my first injection. A week later, I returned for the second. Once again it was after regular office hours. This time, before the actual injection, I felt the doctor doing things that had more to do with his pleasure than with my possible pregnancy. How shocking! I could hardly believe that this elderly physician with a German accent just like my father's would try to take advantage of me. I felt helpless. He had abused my trust, and in my situation, I was completely at his mercy. As he helped me with my coat that second visit, his hand purposely grazed my breast. Rather than react, I held my body stiffly, and pretended not to notice his inappropriate advance. I coldly walked out the door—my poor opinion of the human race had found a new low.

Despite the doctor's abuse, a week later I dutifully returned for my third injection. I was relieved when the final appointment ended without incident. It had been a traumatic series of events, and I could not bring myself to tell anyone what I had been through—especially Del Rio. He was unpredictable, and I was afraid of how he might react in his paranoid state of mind.

Unfortunately, the injections did not work; I was pregnant. What a dilemma! I certainly wasn't anxious to have a baby, especially with a psychotic father. Under the circumstances, I felt my only option was an abortion. Not so easy in 1953. Abortion was illegal and doctors didn't want to risk their professions. Even the abusive doctor I returned to in my desperation, refused to help me.

I had recently started seeing a new psychotherapist, but when I asked her for advice, her response was, "Don't you have some problem with living we could discuss?" I stared at her in disbelief. She went on, "Why don't you come back when you have resolved this situation."

I couldn't bring myself to ask her what could possibly be more pressing than my current dilemma. I was on my own. Cautiously I put out feelers among my restaurant coworkers and was eventually referred to a doctor in Union City, New Jersey. The fee was three hundred dollars. Somehow, I managed to scrape together the money. Then I summoned my courage and made an appointment.

Arriving at the Union City office, I was surprised to find the waiting room full of women. There were elderly women and women with children, plus two obviously pregnant young girls. I was shown into the doctor's office. He got right to the point, "How can I help you?" I explained my situation and pleaded my case: I could not possibly have this baby. The doctor examined me and confirmed the pregnancy before conferring with his nurse for several minutes. He wasted no time, "Do you have the money?" I told him I had three hundred dollars in cash, and he and the nurse led me to another room. Handing me a gown, the nurse instructed me to undress.

It was a windowless room with an examination table in the center, and a small metal stand against one wall. The nurse acted deliberately and put my legs into the stirrups. Shortly after, the doctor entered and quickly began the first part of the procedure, the dilation, followed by the scraping or curettage. There could be no anesthesia in case of a sudden police raid, and the pain was excruciating. The nurse took my hand and tried to soothe me. Between my griping bouts of pain, I heard her say, "There, there. It'll be over soon." I tried to be strong and holdback my screams. The twenty-minute procedure felt like a lifetime.

There was no raid that afternoon, thank goodness. The nurse helped me dress, and I was given fifteen minutes to rest on a cot. Then, without further ado, I was whisked out the door. I headed home with an emergency phone number and two aspirin. Exhausted, I dragged my limp body back to the depot to wait for the next bus to Penn Station. From there, I had to take the subway to 96th Street and Broadway, then walk several more blocks to my apartment.

Evelyn and Marie had moved out a few weeks before my abortion, deathly afraid of Del Rio and his drinking. I hoisted myself into bed and descended into a deep sleep. When I awoke, I was badly in need TLC. Del arrived and I broke. I told him about the pregnancy and the abortion earlier that afternoon. To my surprise, Del remained quite calm as I delivered my tale. Then he quietly left me to rest. Completely worn out by the day's events, I fell back into a deep sleep.

The next thing I felt was the harsh blow of Del's fists against my skull. As he struck me, he yelled and cursed, calling me a whore and worse. I was terrified. "Stop, stop!" I screamed, as I tried to defend myself. Weakened and dazed, the instinct to survive took over like a reflex, and my body turned to the wall on my right and shrank into a fetal position. I shut my eyes and clinched every muscle in my face as hard as I could hoping Del would stop, but he didn't—rage had overtaken him. To this day, I believe Del Rio would have continued to bludgeon me until I lay lifeless had it not been for my faithful dog Rusty. He jumped and nipped relentlessly at Del's legs until Del suddenly seemed to return to his senses. Then, without a word, he turned away from my battered body and walked out of the apartment straight through the door he had just smashed in.

After he left, I called the police, but I couldn't bring myself to press charges. My sympathetic heart was sure this man would never survive jail, and truthfully, I felt partly responsible for his violent outburst—I had destroyed Del's child. I knew his guilt would be burden enough to suffer. Only after the police had left did the shock set into my body. I began to shake like a leaf. My left eye was swollen shut and a huge lump grew on my left temple. Now I realized how right Evelyn and Marie had been about Del. Now, I too, was afraid, scared to death to stay in my basement apartment alone. But there was no one to call; I was too proud and too embarrassed to admit my mistake to my former room-mates.

My father? He was also out of the question. I was sure he would have me arrested if he learned of my pregnancy and the abortion. In desperation, I called Bob Kravitz. Bob was one of my regular customers at my restaurant job. We weren't close, but he lived in the neighborhood—in less than ten minutes he was at my side.

Aghast at my appearance and the demolished front door, he swooped me up with little Rusty by my side and led us to his apartment for the night. Bob offered me the comfort and support I had always craved, but never received from the men in my life. He was caring, and protective, and told me I was welcome to stay with him as long as I needed. Despite his kindness, I still felt like a burden; I had imposed on Bob too much already. After a few days, I returned to my apartment. But Bob continued to look out for me; every night after the incident, he would eat dinner at the restaurant, then walk me home.

Del called to apologize, and we talked. In spite of the

recent trauma and abuse he had inflicted; my demeanor was rational and reasonable. Calm and collected, I informed him I wasn't ready to see him. Looking back, I must have appeared completely unfeeling to this passionate man—devoid of all emotion; that was my way in a crisis—the way my circumstances had conditioned me. My life was built on relationships where I learned I was unworthy, and undeserving of love and respect, leaving me naïve to my vulnerability. Rather than hold Del responsible for his abuse, I dismissed it. I sought to escape my pain through detaching, and I avoided present suffering by intellectualizing.

Two days after I returned home, Bob and I we were sitting and talking over a cup of tea after work when the phone rang. It was the long-distance operator from Findlay. Someone wanted to speak to me; I was asked to "Please hold on." I was excited, expecting this to be Daddy. Maybe he was calling me to reply to the long letter I had sent several weeks earlier, where I once again tried to explain myself to him. I hoped this call might be the beginning of a better understanding between us.

But it wasn't Daddy. On the other end of the line, I heard the voice of my uncle Dwight Murray. "I'm glad I finally reached you; your father had a heart attack yesterday."

I offered to come home right away. I hoped that for once in my life my father might actually need me. But Dwight continued, "I'm sorry Gisela, but he passed away this morning. The funeral will be held on Friday."

I let out a scream. I didn't want to believe the words! My father was only fifty-four and had not been ill. I quickly pulled myself together as Bob tried to comfort me. Never before had I let anyone see me lose control of my emotions.

Bob continued to be a tremendous help—he made the train reservation to Findlay, helped me pack, and even took me to the station the following morning. While I was gone, he offered to keep an eye on my apartment and take care of Rusty and my cat. I don't know what I would have done without him.

On the train, I was still in a daze and not feeling much of anything. I stared out the window, barely conscious of the changing landscape passing by. When I arrived in Findlay, Dwight Murray, my father's friend and lawyer, picked me up from the station and we drove directly to the funeral home. My father's body was already laid out on display in an open coffin, his arms crossed over his chest. Although he had not been a deeply religious man, this was so totally against Jewish tradition that I was horrified.

Without consulting me, I learned that my father's third wife, Marjorie, had already planned the entire funeral. The daughter of a Methodist minister, Marjorie chose a joint religious service, conducted by one of her minister friends and a stand-in rabbi no one knew. I felt lost among Marjorie's nine family members who were all staying at the house. They praised Marjorie's strength and how well she was coping under the circumstances. They showed little compassion for the daughter who had just lost her father. To add insult to injury, the morning after the funeral, Marjorie's mother made some insidious remarks about my father's "race." I couldn't wait to escape these people.

I sat silently and alone amongst all the commotion and left Findlay the day after the funeral; once more I felt numb, dismissed by the world.

The Will

My father and Marjorie had been married just over a year. It seemed thoughtless that she had made all his funeral arrangements before even notifying me of his death. Without my input, Jewish custom had been completely ignored. I felt out of place at my own father's funeral surrounded by this huge family of Methodists that had descended on my house.

Before his death, my father had promised his sister Gerda that he would come to England when Marga, their older sister, was near death. After his death, I felt that it was my place to go in his stead. So, the day after the funeral, I took the train back to New York and prepared to travel to England. Once again, my friend Bob was fantastic: he reserved my plane ticket, arranged for an emergency passport, and wrapped up loose ends. I left for England.

Just two weeks after my father's death, Marga succumbed to the colon cancer she had long been battling. Gerda was devastated. Her two remaining siblings were gone within a two-week period. I was glad that I had come to help. Gerda reacted to her loss with a series of illnesses and I felt I couldn't leave her. I was now her only immediate family.

I did everything I could to please her, but she was always surprised to find that the peas were hulled, the spinach washed, and the potatoes peeled when she came upstairs from the surgery for lunch. She must have been shocked that my father had been able to civilize the girl she had once dismissed as: "Just like her mother."

Gerda was beautiful and ambitious. Right after her apprenticeship, she had joined a private dental practice in Düsseldorf. When Jews were no longer allowed to practice medicine or dentistry in Germany, she immigrated to England, where she established a practice. She arranged for Marga to join her from Düsseldorf, and after the Kristallnacht in 1938, she brought my grandmother to England as well. Aunt Gerda had devoted herself to her profession and her family, neglecting any social life that might have led to marriage. By the time I arrived in England in 1954, she had become every bit the British spinster: outfitted in tweeds, walking shoes, hat, and umbrella—Always alone.

I spent five months with Gerda in Bournemouth while she recovered from the loss of her siblings and the illnesses that followed. But eventually, I needed to be back in Findlay for the probate of my father's will; I was his main heir. Except for specific sums left to his two sisters, I was to inherit the entire estate, including the house. The total value when combined was estimated to be nearly $250,000. In 1954, this was a lot of money.

Upon returning to the States, I spent a few days in New York repacking and collecting the necessary papers. I arrived in Findlay a few days before the six months probate period expired. Dwight Murray picked me up at the train station and took me to the local hotel. I was surprised; I had assumed that I would be staying in the house I had inherited. "Dwight, I don't want to stay in the local hotel where all the traveling salesmen hang out. I want to stay at my house."

Dwight was slow to respond. Finally, he replied, "I was away when Marjorie moved out, and she took a few more pieces of furniture than she was supposed to. The house might not be so comfortable for you."

I was stubborn and insisted. "Dwight, I don't care. Just take me to the house!"

We left the hotel and headed to Dwight's office to pick up the house keys and drove down Main Street to the cul-de-sac where the house was located.

Dwight opened the front door and I couldn't believe what I saw—or rather what I didn't see! No couch, no tables or chairs, no lamps. The piano stood alone in the living room. I walked through the entire house and quickly understood why Dwight didn't want me to see it. All the rooms were empty: the bedrooms, the dining room, even the sunroom. In the kitchen, only the disconnected pipes stuck out of the wall, a reminder of where the washing machine, dryer, dishwasher, stove, and refrigerator had once stood.

Marjorie had signed a prenuptial agreement, which stated that she was not entitled to anything my father owned, but she was permitted to take any furniture they had purchased while together. I was only interested in the old pieces with sentimental value, but now it was all gone.

"Dwight! How could you let her take everything? You are the executor of the estate; you drew up the prenuptial agreement. This isn't right. I was gracious enough to let her stay in the house and use one of the cars until the end of the school year to avoid disrupting the lives of her children, and this is how she repays me! Take me to see her right now!"

Back in town, Dwight dropped me off in front of Marjorie's townhouse—It was on the same street where he lived with his family. I rang the bell. The girls greeted me by my middle name— "Ruthie dear, what a surprise! How lovely to see you."

Marjorie invited me to sit on the couch that should have been in my house. I said coldly, "I came to retrieve a chair, a table, and a lamp, so that I can stay in the house while I'm in Findlay."

Marjorie replied, "I'm sorry, but I can't do that. It would not be legal to make changes before the will has been probated. I hope you appreciate the fact that I left the piano for you and two beds in the attic."

An awkward silence followed, before she added, "Ruthie, did you try to find your mother while you were in Europe?"

"No, I didn't. I figured there were already two wives after my father's money and I didn't need a third one to battle."

"Tsk, tsk, Ruthie, have you seen your psychiatrist lately?"

With this, I stormed out of the townhouse and walked to the nearest bus stop. Back at the house, I dismantled one of the beds in the attic and carried it downstairs, one piece at a time, to the large living room, the only room with carpeting and drapes. Both had been peed on numerous times by my father's Scottish terriers. There were no linens, but I was tired out. I fell onto the mattress and eventually into an uneasy sleep.

The next day, I took the bus to town and went shopping. I carted home a hotplate, an old-fashioned icebox, some towels, and a set of sheets. From the local market I bought soap, food for breakfast and lunch, and an orange crate. At the same time, I arranged for a small block of ice for my new ice box to be delivered on a regular basis.

A couple of days later, a former patient of my father's brought me two table lamps he had salvaged from my father's office. He had heard that I was living in an empty house and decided that I needed the lamps. My high school friend, Doris, offered me the use of an upholstered chair, and suddenly the house felt quite cozy. I ate a hot meal in town at lunchtime and kept cereal, milk, cold cuts, and butter in my icebox. Most of the time I spent going through my father's old letters and photos in the attic.

Then disaster struck. The buses went on strike. I had no way to get into town. I asked Dwight to drive me one day, and as he brought me home, he suggested, "Why don't you buy a car—you can afford it." But I couldn't drive; I had never learned. Dwight was adamant. "I'll see what I can do."

On the following Monday a salesman appeared with a beautiful Chevy—a dark blue Bel Air, with a snowy white top.

"Teach me how to drive and I'll buy it!" I promised.

The salesman agreed. On Monday through Friday, he gave me one-hour lessons on the ways of the road. On Thursday afternoon, Dwight's wife accompanied me while I drove on the nearby highway. In between, I practiced parallel parking in my driveway.

From the first moment, I felt at home behind the wheel of this car. After my last Friday lesson, my instructor followed me to town so that I could take the driver's test: I passed with flying colors. Proud of myself and tired of being stuck in Findlay, I called my old college roommate Elsa and set out on the 150-mile drive to Detroit that same afternoon. It was a pleasure to take the car up to seventy miles an hour on the highway. Merely sitting in bumper-to-bumper traffic on a six-lane avenue in the middle of "Motor City" during Friday afternoon rush hour made me nervous, but I finally made it to Elsa's house. After a pleasant weekend with Elsa and her husband, I drove back to Findlay on Monday morning without incident.

At a quarter of five on the last day the will could be contested, Dwight Murray was served with papers doing just that. Marjorie claimed that the prenuptial agreement she had signed was not valid. Her declared assets valued $150,000 at the time of the agreement; my father's assets came to $250,000. So now, according to Ohio law, she, the widow, and I, the only child, were each entitled to half the estate.

Dwight Murray already represented the estate as the named executor. Marjorie also had her own lawyer. I needed to find representation. I picked a lawyer who had a reputation for being very independent, and only later did I discover he was Dwight Murray's first cousin.

When I first heard that Marjorie had contested the will, I wanted to fight her tooth and nail. My father had been very specific about his last wishes, and I was determined to carry them out. He must have suspected that Marjorie was marrying him for his money, and he insisted on the prenuptial agreement. And I had been very generous, I thought, by not demanding back the furniture.

I figured I would have to stay in Findlay for a long fight, so two weeks after my weekend in Detroit, I decided to drive the eight hundred miles back to New York City to pick up my dog

Rusty and some clothes. It was a very long drive, but on the way back I had Rusty for company.

Back in Findlay, Rusty and I visited every interesting landmark in northern Ohio in the AAA guidebook. We would go for the day, along with lunch and my painting supplies. Once in a while, I stopped to paint a scene I found appealing. In Findlay I made a life for myself. I explored the new shopping malls on the outskirts of town, checked out the library, and took an evening art class at the high school.

When I joined the cast of the Elk's 1954 annual musical production, life in Findlay became much more interesting. One of the guys in the show, Hal, asked me out. We always had to go to a neighboring town for dinner or a movie because Hal was in the middle of a custody battle—he didn't want to be seen dating. His wife had come out as a lesbian and he wanted custody of their daughter.

He happened to own a Chevy Bel Air in brown and white, but "in the dark they all look the same," he said. He always made sure he was gone from my driveway by daylight. Our relationship made life in Findlay quite bearable.

Marjorie and I were not on speaking terms. I was angry and had decried her at every opportunity. Now everyone knew about her deceit and how I had arrived home to find an empty house. Findlay was buzzing with gossip.

Dwight Murray was obviously a bad lawyer; his work was full of weaknesses. It was Dwight who had drawn up my father's will, drafted the prenuptial agreement, and submitted my father's tax returns for the last twelve years of his life. When the will was contested, a critical error was revealed between the declared value on the prenuptial agreement and the amount of yearly income tax my father paid—the numbers did not match, and the IRS quickly noticed the discrepancy. After further investigation, the estate was charged a whopping $95,000 for back taxes and fines. After paying Dwight, Marjorie's lawyer, and my lawyer $30,000 each, a mere $65,000 thousand remained for Marjorie and me to bicker over. If we split it, we would each end up with about $30,000 and the lawyers would have to stop licking their chops.

Marjorie was always trying to show how concerned she was about me. Once, she invited me to a luncheon at the Findlay Country Club. To her surprise I decided to accept. After we finished eating, I stood up and said, "Thank you so much for inviting me today, a privilege my parents never enjoyed." I stopped to marvel at the discomfort I had just created. Then I took a deep breath and continued, "I thought you might be interested to know that I have decided to settle my father's will out of court."

It was a pleasure to see the disbelief on Marjorie's face and the shock that rippled through the waspish country clubbers listening in. Findlay's gossip circle was disappointed the cat fighting had come to an end. A few days later I packed up my car and Rusty and drove the eight hundred miles back to New York.

In retrospect, I realize that I always had trouble accepting money from my father. When the business with Marjorie and the will began, I could have consulted Rose Cone, one of the cousins that first sponsored my father in the United States. She was a retired lawyer, living in Cleveland. She knew the Ohio state law and would have gladly advised me. In the end, I went on with my life in New York, with enough money to pay for my tuition at Juilliard.

The Singing

"You have such a beautiful voice."

These are the words I heard from everyone who heard me sing, and with this encouragement, I developed a secret ambition to become a singer. At the University of Michigan, I took a music appreciation course that introduced me to classical music. What an experience! The melodies filled me with wonder and intense emotion, and I fell madly in love with all the composers I heard, but especially Beethoven. Now, more than ever, I wanted to become an opera singer.

When I first came to New York, I made some feeble attempts at studying voice. However, I had neither the time nor the money to continue, so singing remained a dream. Now, in 1954, I was thirty years old, my father had died, and I had inherited his entire estate. Dwight Murray had assured me that my inheritance would enable me to do anything I wanted without the need to earn a living—I could realize my dream of becoming an opera singer or so it seemed.

I soon learned a dream is not enough; you also need the necessary talent. After singing for the head of the voice department at Columbia University, I was strongly encouraged to take time for further vocal studies. As I already had an academic degree, the department head suggested that I audition to enter the music diploma course at Juilliard. Over the summer, one of Juilliard's voice teachers taught me the required audition pieces. I was unaware that I was applying to one of the top music conservatories in the country. It was all about convenience for me: I lived a short bus ride away from Juilliard, then located on 122nd Street.

Only after I was accepted into the program did I realize that I was competing with people who had been studying music since they were four years old. Here I was at age thirty-two, not even able to read music.

In my first year, I was assigned the same voice teacher with whom I had worked over the summer. Although excited and eager to finally be studying voice, I couldn't stand this voice teacher. She had never been a singer herself and was insensitive as a teacher, accompanist, and person. Not only that, since I had ended up with barely enough money from my father's estate to cover the tuition at Juilliard, I had to work to support myself, buy my books, and also my music. My blue-haired "Madame" of a vocal coach had no compassion for my situation.

Thank goodness, in my second year, I was allowed to switch teachers. I now studied with a famous German lieder singer. I was dedicated and worked diligently, learning everything she suggested, but I struggled with the vocal control needed to sing lieder. Toward the end of my third year, during a particularly exasperating lesson, Mme. Leonard sighed, "Gisela, I don't think you have a talent for singing."

I was completely taken aback. I felt that she was wrong

about my talent for singing, but also partly right, for I had a problem with my voice. I had worked hard to catch up with my music studies and figured this new teacher would help me with my vocal problems. Only much later did I realize that one goes to Juilliard to learn interpretation, repertoire, and performing skills, and to make professional connections. You're expected to have mastered your instrument prior to attending the school. It is not the place for learning basic technique! I continued to fight and found an outside teacher to supplement my studies, but after almost two years, my voice failed to improve—I couldn't capture the nuance a vocalist requires. There was a noticeable break between registers, and my lower register was no louder than a mouse. I was confused, upset, and totally frustrated—what had happened to the voice everyone used to call so beautiful?

My last year at Juilliard, I contracted a severe upper respiratory infection and was referred to a doctor who specialized in treating singers. After listening to me and examining my vocal equipment he pronounced, "Miss Selo, I don't understand how you are able to sing at all. You have a veil over your nasopharynx." At my second appointment, we discovered the nature of the veil—It was identified as scar tissue.

Only then did I remember the chronic throat infections that began when I was sixteen, and the multiple nasopharyngeal surgeries, and the complications that followed. How could I have known that so many surgeries would cause the formation of excess scar tissue, then a nasopharyngeal obstruction and an alteration in my airway that permanently interfered with the resonance in my vocal cords? In spite of my handicap, I pursued my dream and sang for twenty years. There were many colorful memories: My first summer in New York, I sang in the chorus of the Chautauqua Opera. Another fabulous summer, I spent at the music school in Aspen, Colorado, and the following summer at Tanglewood studying opera with Boris Goldovsky. Over the years, I was paid to perform at weddings and small concerts. For ten years, I was the soprano soloist in a church, and for fifteen years I was part of an adult quartet, accompanying a boys' choir and famous cantors in the Catskills. With the Amato Opera Company in the fifties, I learned and performed about twenty major soprano roles. I even had the opportunity to sing Beethoven's *Ninth Symphony* under Leonard Bernstein! Although my acting ability and my innate musicality carried me a long way, I was perpetually aware of my inadequacies and the frustration they brought me.

Singing ignited my passion and creative fire—my years at Juilliard were an especially expansive time in my life. I met George, a fellow student and violin prodigy turned viola player, majoring in conducting. George was twelve years my junior, but we were drawn together by powerful forces—a shared love for music and driving intellectual curiosity. Our fire thrived for two wonderful years. It was the most stimulating and satisfying relationship of my entire life. But eventually, our romance faded. George left for Paris on scholarship where he met a young female music student. When he returned to New York, he had changed toward me—our shared values could no longer bridge the generational gap between us.

After I graduated from Juilliard, I found a well-renowned vocal coach and made one last attempt to improve my vocal inadequacies. After several lessons, it was clear that he too could not help. The time had come to quit singing altogether. I'd had enough!

Painful as it was to admit failure, I accepted my reality—I could never become the world-renowned opera singer of my dreams. At the same time, it was also a relief to be free of the sleepless nights before, and total frustration after, every performance. Had I realized that I was dealing with a pathology, I would surely have dreamed a different dream. Nevertheless, I have no regrets about investing so many years, so much effort, and so much money in my dreams of becoming a singer. The twenty years I devoted to this passion gave me a sense of purpose, and a reason for living that I had not had before. And when in the end I did give up singing, my love for music remained. Music has been, and still is, the greatest joy of my life. It has sustained me through the years; the light during times of loneliness and depression.

Home Again

For more than forty years, I had been living in Old Howard Beach, New York. In all that time, I never felt a sense of belonging. Now, back in Germany, interacting with lively, intelligent, and friendly people, I asked myself, Could I live here in Germany, in this town where I was born?

The West Germany city of Krefeld, set on the Rhine, had invited the surviving Jewish immigrants for a reunion. I had accepted, and, since I was traveling by myself, I opted to stay with a host family, the Kassels. When I arrived, I was immediately received with genuine warmth and affection. For my entire ten-day stay, I was treated as one of the family. I felt as if I were among friends, peers, people who shared my interests! The Kassels had taken me along to visit their friends, and I felt a sense of community I had never before experienced—Is this where I truly belonged?

With my mother having passed away, I felt the desire to see my half-brother, Wolfgang. He still lived in Düsseldorf, a tram ride away from Krefeld. He had remained in Germany throughout the war and as a result, bore both the physical and psychological scars of war. His decision to remain in Germany condemned him to a life of struggle.

On the day I was to visit Wolfgang, the Kassels brought me to the tram station in Krefeld. Wolfgang met me in Düsseldorf, and we spent a very pleasant afternoon together, walking and talking. I was delighted to see how much we resembled one another—I felt instantly connected to him.

By four o'clock, it was time to return to Krefeld. Wolfgang walked me back to the station, where we shared a tearful goodbye before I boarded the tram. It had been an exhausting day—after all the walking, my back was aching. On the train, there was a single seat available, and I plopped myself down, relieved to at last be off my feet. The tram was crowded, and I realized that if I got up to pay the fare up front, I would lose my seat. I couldn't face standing for the entire trip, so I held on to the fare and figured I would pay when I exited the tram.

About twenty minutes into the forty-five-minute ride, a uniformed, heavy-set female inspector boarded the train and began to check receipts. When she arrived at my seat, I explained in German (still pretty good after so many years), "I mistakenly got on at the wrong entrance and there was just one seat left. I have a bad back and standing causes me a lot of pain."

I showed her the fare clutched in my hand and added, "I'll pay on my way out."

"I will take the money now, plus an additional fine of forty," she said scowling.

"I gave all my money to my brother in Düsseldorf. I'm an American citizen here on a short visit."

Some instinct told me not to mention that I was one of the

Jewish refugees, here at the invitation of the city.

"Show me your passport!" She barked.

"Please, I didn't bring my papers—it was such a short trip."

"You should always carry your ID with you. I am placing you under arrest. You will accompany me to the nearest police station."

Since I still spoke German like a Rhinelander, she must have thought I was not American. She obviously did not believe me, but I really didn't think she would arrest me; it wasn't as if I had refused to pay the fare.

Now, just as a Nazi officer does in the movies, she planted herself menacingly in front of me, legs apart and arms folded over her broad chest as she watched me like a hawk. As we got near the last stop, most of the passengers had gotten off, and she took the seat across from me, continuing her accusing stare. Although I knew I had done nothing wrong, she made me feel like a criminal. I lowered my gaze under the discomfort of her squinty, judgmental eyes, and tight-lipped mouth. She must have thought that she had bagged a hardened criminal or perhaps even an international spy. When we reached the end of the line, she ordered, "Follow me and don't try to escape."

She then marched me, single file, to the nearby police station and reluctantly turned me over to the police captain. Luckily, the captain understood the situation. He dismissed the tram inspector and called the Kassels. After confirming my story, the Kassels were able to pick me up, and we returned to their home.

That incident brought home to me how I was now a citizen of a free society in the United States. I realized once and for all I could never again live under such a strict, authoritarian regime. Despite enjoying my time with the Kassels, I was now gladder than ever to be an American—I was grateful to be going home to the "land of the free."

The Crack in the Wall

A heavy hand came down on my right shoulder as I was trying to push open the metal door of Alexander's department store that exited onto 58th Street in New York. "Please accompany us to the office," a male voice spoke behind me. The hand remained on my shoulder, guiding me firmly through the crowd of shoppers. Outwardly, I was calm, but boy, my heart was pounding. Once inside the store's office, I saw that the man and woman in uniform who had escorted me in, were now guarding the door. I faced a man at a desk who was busily writing on a yellow pad. After a few minutes, he looked up and said politely, "Would you please empty your pockets?"

I pulled out my keys, a few subway tokens, some crumpled tissues, and finally, the small red scarf I had taken from one of the store's big display tables.

"Do you have a receipt for that scarf, Miss? A witness saw you removing it from a display table."

I knew then that I had been caught. There was no escaping the fact that I had taken the scarf. I decided that my best defense was honesty. I began to speak, "I'm very sorry. I don't really know why I took the scarf. You see, kleptomania has been one of my problems. In fact, it's one of the reasons I am in psychotherapy. I'm actually on my way to the therapist now." I gave him my therapist's name and number, and while I stood there, he called Mrs. Morgan to confirm my statement. She apparently did so, for I was permitted to leave with just a warning this time. "Don't ever try this again, Miss. Next time you will be arrested."

As fast as I could, I ran from that office; I was so relieved the officer had been lenient with me. It was the first time I had been caught. Looking back, getting caught was what I needed to end my nasty habit. Since the age of twelve, I had gotten away with stealing from stores. I was now fifty-one. The hardest part came next—facing my therapist. I had no excuse for my stealing.

She confronted me as soon as I entered her office, "Gisela, why did you do this?"

Ashamed, I looked away and shrugged. A shy, "I don't know," passed through my lips.

"Gisela, you did this deliberately to hurt me."

"No I didn't," I protested. "It had nothing to do with you."

"Yes, it did," she retorted. Then quietly added, "And you know what? You succeeded." Stunned, I looked up at her. I could see the hurt in her eyes. Prior to that day, she had never shown any emotion. I knew a therapist was supposed to stay uninvolved with clients—keep a professional distance. Shock overtook me and I was speechless. Until this moment, I had been totally unaware that anything I did or said had an impact on another human being.

When my father took me from my mother at age five and called me unwanted, I guess I couldn't deal with the deep hurt. I covered my pain with a protective coating. After so many years of feeling unloved and unwanted by my father and stepmother, that protective coating had grown and thickened into a cold, hard, concrete wall. And how well the wall had worked. Nothing could penetrate my shield; I thought I was safe from hurt. The trouble was, the wall had shut out not only hurt and pain, but also anger, anxiety, guilt, shame, compassion, trust, and love. It had completely isolated me emotionally, so that I felt no connection to humanity and the world surrounding me. My life had been an emotional vacuum.

But in an instant, an epiphany happened! I was suddenly confronted with a new found awareness: I had hurt someone that I cared about. I left my therapy session that day in a daze, my head spinning. Disoriented, I boarded a train, not realizing that I was headed in the wrong direction, the Bronx instead of Queens! Eventually I made it home, but without my pocketbook.

All my life, I thought insight was one of my strengths; now, here I was confronted with my total lack of it. There is insight and then there is behavior. It took me years to understand that intellectual insight is only a first step; it does not result in behavioral change. For the first time, I was seeing myself as others probably saw me: cold and uncaring, without empathy, understanding, or compassion. I was often verbally cruel when it was totally uncalled for, and my body language effectively told people to stay away. I shrank from feeling and intimacy apparently ignored other peoples' feelings. In fact, until that day, I had not even realized that other people had feelings!

For days, these thoughts raced through my head. As I started to rise out of my initial fog, I had another amazing revelation: I did not want to remain an empty shell. Slowly, I started to pull myself together and follow a new path with an opening heart. I tried to become more aware of what I said and did and how it affected others, but it was difficult to change. Like anything meaningful in life, it required work. I had to be a warrior and break down the walls I had built around myself.

It took ten years of working with Mrs. Morgan before I was ready to leave therapy. But the work had paid off, for now I was able to get angry, feel hurt, and respond appropriately to my emotions. My conscience had developed as I let myself freely experience empathy, guilt, and anxiety. I had begun to grow into an adult and could now deal with my problems without the help of a therapist.

Originally diagnosed as a sociopath, and given up on as hopeless by previous therapists, I shall be forever grateful to Mrs. Morgan for her perception and endless patience. I know that without her help, I would never have managed to change as I did, to go through that slow and frustrating growth process that began with the crack in the wall.

Story of a Marriage

My car had a flat. I saw it as I was walking the dogs past my parking spot. After taking them home, I came back to the car to change the tire, something I had done numerous times. Unfortunately, this time my spare was flat too. Thank goodness, there was a gas station right across the street. I approached the attendant; his name tag said "Eddie."

"I can't leave the station unattended, miss, but if you come back at midnight, I can help you."

I lived only two blocks away and came back at midnight. Eddie was finishing his shift. I watched him as he rolled each tire to the station, fixed the flats, and then put one tire back on the car and the other in the trunk.

Eddie refused payment, so to show my gratitude, I invited him to have coffee at Bickfords, an all-night restaurant nearby. He was a very good-looking man—slender, but with the broad shoulders and muscular arms of a someone accustomed to physical work. He was shy and said very little, but what nice guy! From then on, I made sure he was on duty when I stopped for gas. Eddie took notice. It wasn't long before he asked me out to dinner. On our first date at a Chinese restaurant, he ordered the only dish he was familiar with: fried rice. Over the next few weeks he took me to the movies and to dinner several times. I was impressed by his gentlemen-like qualities and behavior in contrast to an obvious lack of education.

It wasn't long before we went to my apartment for coffee. The mutual attraction and our chemistry were undeniable. But it was complicated. He confessed early on that he was married and had a son. The story was he stayed married only because of his son, and he owned his house and was still fixing it up. One day he had come home from work early to find his two-year-old son barefoot and in diapers outside playing, while his wife was drinking in the corner bar with some guy. From that day on, as far as he was concerned, his marriage was over.

We began to spend as much time together as possible, and I grew to love and respect him. There was something different about Eddie—he was open and honest and didn't play games. He was not in the least bit materialistic or conscious of status; he couldn't care less about what the Joneses' had or the neighbors thought. These were values we both shared. I was impressed by his sense of responsibility, and although he was very protective, he was never controlling. A simple, hardworking, kind, decent, handsome guy with gorgeous legs. He had quit the gas station and was now driving a cab. I was freelancing as a photo colorist at the time and could adjust my schedule to his. We used to meet in the parking lot at 96th Street and Riverside Drive, eat lunch, talk, and smooch.

Eddie was one of six—five brothers and a sister. He lived in Throgs Neck in the Bronx, just around the corner from his parents' house on the Sound. In his spare time, he would still swim and fish there. After obtaining a legal separation from his wife, he moved back home with his parents.

Eddie's mother didn't like me. She never forgave Eddie for dumping his wife Joanie, and she eyed me suspiciously as the cause for the break-up. Eddie's father, Solomon Cohn, was a caretaker in a Protestant church; he would appear for meals, then quickly disappear.

Mrs. Cohn had skin like porcelain, and a shock of long white hair, but her mouth and nose were grotesquely deformed. One of Eddie's sisters-in-law told me that his mother was born with a harelip to a British father and an East Indian mother. The harelip was considered a sign of the devil in those days, and her father had viciously beaten her with a lead pipe. Once I caught a glimpse of her badly scarred legs. If the story were true, it was not surprising that she was both mean and paranoid. There was something uncomfortable in the air when I went to the Cohns to see Eddie.

I was uneasy with Mrs. Cohn—she and Eddie argued often about me. On one occasion, she threw all his clothes out on the street. After this, he moved in with me. In spite of our differences, we were pretty happy together. Neither one of us had close friends, but we had each other and our dogs.

Occasionally, we socialized with one of his brothers, but more often we found ourselves with his only sister Jenny, quite a remarkable lady—a polio survivor, but unstoppable. She had been Eddie's only caretaker in his younger years. She was married to Paul—also stricken with polio as a child—who owned an insurance agency. Jenny, in spite of the braces on her arms and legs, managed to run their three-story house. She had given birth to a brain-damaged girl, who was unable to walk or feed herself. Jenny refused to put her in a home and took care of that child until she died at the age of seven. I had the utmost respect for both Paul and Jenny.

On Sundays we would pick up Eddie Jr. at his mother's in the Bronx and take him out for the day. I found him ill-mannered and greedy, but we tried to show him a good time. Eventually, Eddie proposed marriage. When I kept putting him off, he finally gave me an ultimatum, "If you won't marry me, I'll get out of your life."

I knew he had a point. After all, we had been going together for five years. But marriage? I knew damn well that we didn't have enough in common to sustain a successful marriage. I also was vaguely aware that I had lingering commitment issues. But I couldn't bear to lose his love. I needed to talk this out with someone, so I decided to consult one of my former therapists from the William Alanson White Institute.

"You might as well face it, Gisela, there is a big hole where your emotions should be," the therapist told me. "At best you can patch the hole over, but you will never be able to fill it. Be grateful that you have found a decent man who wants to marry you. Better than you could have hoped for. By all means, marry him."

And I did.

Joanie, his first wife, didn't care about being divorced, as long as Eddie paid child support. She had actually tried to pin another pregnancy on him, but Eddie Jr., when questioned, assured the court judge that "Uncle Harry" was always nice to him when he slept over. The child even had a photograph of Uncle Harry embracing his mother. Eddie won his case.

We figured out that an uncontested divorce with no

custody issues was much cheaper and quicker in Mexico. So we decided to take my little Volkswagen and drive there. I mapped out the most direct route, and we took turns driving the two thousand miles over five days. We stopped in small out-of-the-way motels and diners along the way. Since Eddie had never been outside of New York, this was quite an adventure for him.

Eddie's prearranged appointment with a lawyer in Juarez went off without a hitch. The very next day, he was a free man. I had wanted to see Acapulco, so we drove there and spent two days in an inexpensive hotel on the Mexican side of town. We had a fabulous room with a balcony overlooking the beach. Presumed to be newlyweds, we were treated royally by the hotel and received a free dinner and wine. We swam and ate and made love. Everything was perfect. I assumed Eddie felt the same way, although I never thought to ask him. Looking back, I realize I rarely asked him anything; he just went along with whatever I planned. But he didn't seem to mind.

On the trip back, we visited Mexico City, where we stayed with my old boyfriend George's parents and attended a bullfight. On the drive back to New York, we took a tour through the Carlsbad Caverns in New Mexico and stopped to have a fabulous shrimp dinner in Brownsville, Texas. Sexually everything was great between us; this was always the highlight of our relationship.

Then something changed. Only a day or so away from New York City, Eddie was behind the wheel. We had been fooling around in the car. I spotted an abandoned house on the side of the road and we pulled over. We grabbed a blanket, and then cleared a place to lie down on the wooden floor. For the first time, I suddenly found myself recoiling from Eddie's touch. The more he tried, the more I froze. I was in tears, but I simply could no longer bear being touched in a sexual way. After an hour or so, we gave up and returned to the car—Eddie frustrated, and I in despair. I assured him that I loved him, but he wouldn't even talk to me.

This problem had plagued me before—in my first marriage and all my serious relationships. Previously, I had attributed it to being with the wrong guy, unaware that I was the source of the problem. Writing this, I feel how terrible my constant sexual rejection must have felt to Eddie, and I regret the pain I must have caused him.

For the next few weeks we were busy getting ready for our wedding at City Hall. Any misgivings I had over marrying Eddie, I pushed away. I couldn't bring myself to call it off. My aunt Klare was fond of Eddie and arranged a lovely wedding dinner for us. When we were first married, Aunt Klare loaned Eddie the money to buy a big truck so he could be an independent long-distance driver. He was often gone for a week at a time, eating and sleeping on the road. This life of a distance driver was hard, and Eddie wasn't cut out for it. I used some of my inheritance to place a down payment on a taxicab medallion. The hours driving a cab were longer, but the money was good. I had graduated from Juilliard by the time we got married and was pursuing a career as a singer, auditioning here and there and booking small jobs, but without much pay.

Eddie was pained watching us pay rent over the years and having nothing to show for it. He insisted on buying a house. We checked out ads for two-family homes, and after weeks of searching, we found the ideal house on an inlet off Jamaica Bay in old Howard Beach. We literally scraped the money together for a second mortgage and signed the deed. We moved in stages with his brother's help, but my long, curved couch would not fit into or even on top of the elevator. Nor could it be maneuvered around the curve of the stairs. My expensive modern couch ended up in pieces in various city dumpsters. The house represented the finality of the commitment I had made, and it felt like the end rather than the beginning of a new life to me.

I became severely depressed and mindlessly went through the motions of everyday life. The pattern set up in that abandoned house on our way back from Mexico continued. My sexual withdrawal became almost total. I dreaded going to bed, anticipating the silent battle, but I resisted Eddie's love with every nerve and muscle of my body, my fingernails digging into my palms. Once, in angry frustration, Eddie put his fist through the bedroom door; every time I looked at that hole, I was reminded of my inadequacy; I finally covered up the hole with a long Chinese calendar.

By this time, we each followed our own pursuits most of the time. I was rehearsing with the Amato Opera Company, and he would take out the cab around 2:00 p.m. I kept house, did the laundry, tended the garden, and when Eddie came home around 2:00 a.m., his dinner was always ready.

Eddie developed stomach ulcers. Stress, the doctor said. Looking back, I wonder if it was only driving a cab in New York City that gave him stomach pains. In any case, we looked for something else he might do. My brother-in-law from London offered him a job in his Manhattan office, but Eddie could barely read, and I knew he couldn't handle an office job.

We investigated ads for gas station franchises. From what was left of my inheritance, I supplied the down payment, and Eddie took over a Shell station in Far Rockaway. Unfortunately, he was not manager material. He lacked imagination and was afraid to spend extra money. Instead of hiring a competent mechanic, he did all the work himself, taking much too long to complete a job. As a result, he lost customers instead of building up a clientele. He was spending long hours at the station and still driving the cab. Eventually he hired a young kid to service the gas pumps in the evening. It was a big mistake. Customers saw a gang of kids hanging out at the station at night. They were scared to stop for gas. Eddie didn't want me to come to the station, and we drifted even further apart. That was the beginning of the end of our marriage.

The Betrayal

In my childhood, I had learned not to trust anybody; commitment was incredibly frightening to me. So, once I made the total commitment of marriage, something had to go. In my case, it was sex. In every other way I was an affectionate and supportive wife: I prepared the meals, did the laundry, cleaned the house, and took care of the garden. But I had absolutely no control over the physical aversion I felt when my husband tried to arouse me. He tried so hard. He was patient and loving, but I could only cringe. I would have given anything, if I could have responded to him like I did during the years before we were married.

Eddie was a simple, straightforward guy, honest, hardworking, and caring, but practically illiterate, and not very articulate. His way of expressing his love for me was primarily sexual, and I was depriving him of that by constantly shrinking from him. I tried to explain that I couldn't help it, but he was not capable of understanding that, and our relationship steadily deteriorated.

We had been married about three years, and although I was

seeing a therapist, the sexual withdrawal did not improve, and Eddie was losing his patience. I couldn't even offer a reasonable explanation; I simply said, "I'm sorry, I just can't."

One day Eddie dropped an innocent remark (or maybe it wasn't so innocent): "You know, I don't have any sexual problems with anybody else."

Although he had been married once before, I didn't think that he was referring to that, and I got very suspicious. Eddie was now operating a Shell station in Far Rockaway. He worked long hours, but when I offered to help with the paperwork, I sensed that he didn't want me around the station. My suspicion grew. The station was located on Central Avenue, one of the main thoroughfares between Queens and Long Island. From Howard Beach one could get there via Nassau County, and head west, or take the Cross Bay Toll Bridge and head east.

One afternoon I drove to Far Rockaway and parked out of sight but where I could still observe the station. While Eddie was busy with a customer inside, I walked by on the opposite side of the street and surveyed the area. There was a laundromat right across from the gas station, just what I needed. Eddie usually took the toll-free route to work, so I took the toll bridge and parked out of sight on the Nassau County side of Central Avenue. Fully prepared, with dirty laundry and a box of detergent, I walked into the busy laundromat and parked myself on the bench right in front of the big glass window. In my long raincoat, babushka, and dark glasses, I was not recognizable, yet I could see everything that was going on at the gas station.

Eddie rented out a few parking spaces on his lot and I watched as cars pulled into park or to get gas. At a quarter to nine, a blue sedan pulled in from the Nassau County side. A slender woman in a blue dress got out and went into the office, carrying a bag from *Dunkin Donuts*. After about ten minutes she came back out accompanied by Eddie, who walked her to the edge of the station. From their body language I could see that she was more than just a customer. She waved to him as she continued walking west on Central Avenue and disappeared into the business district of Far Rockaway. From the laundromat, I was not able to see where she went, so after a few minutes, I went back to my car and drove home without even doing the laundry.

Before nine the next morning, I found a parking place on Central Avenue in the Far Rockaway business district. Looking east, I could just see a blue dress emerging from the gas station, walking towards me and going into the local bank.

I headed home, took Eddie's business bank book and drove back to Far Rockaway. At the bank, I spotted the teller with the blue dress and that's the line I stood in. I took a good look at her. Nothing special, I thought. I pushed the bank book under the glass partition and said slowly and clearly, "I think my husband made a mistake in his bank book; would you check the last deposit please."

She took one look at the name on the bank book, turned bright red, excused herself, and hurriedly walked away from the window. A few minutes later she came back, now quite composed, and said, "The balance is correct. There is no mistake."

That's what you think, I thought to myself. To her I said, "Thank you very much."

I drove back to Howard Beach, quite pleased with myself. I hadn't been home more than a half hour, when Eddie came storming into house. "What did you do? If you make her lose her job, I'll never forgive you!"

I answered quietly, "What did I do? I thought there was a mistake in your bank book, and I went to check it out. I can't help it if your girlfriend feels so guilty that she got all upset facing your wife." He left without another word. Eddie didn't come home that night. I assumed he was with her. When he came home the next evening, he said he had spent the night at the station. We ate dinner in silent misery.

Then, I couldn't take it anymore. I said, "We can't go on like this. It's either me or her."

Eddie looked uncertain and remained mute for several agonizing minutes.

"I'll have to let you know," he said, and with that strutted out to his car and took off into the night. He didn't come home for the next four nights.

In my mind I was quite sure he didn't want to leave me. But if this were true, why was he hesitating? I couldn't stand the suspense any longer. I drove to the gas station. He was busy with a customer but promised he would come home after work. About 9:00 p.m. he got home, took a shower, shaved, and then sat down in his easy chair. He still hadn't said a word. Finally, I asked him outright, "Well, what did you decide?"

He hemmed and hawed, and finally came out with, "She's pregnant. I have to take care of that first."

I stared at him and then something in me snapped. I screamed, "Get out, get out! Right now! Out!"

He tried to say something, but I wouldn't listen. I, who had never been able to feel angry before, was beside myself with fury. I kept screaming, "Get out, get out—if you don't get out,

I'll call the police!"

I started pummeling his back with my fists, but he wouldn't budge or even defend himself. I picked up the phone and called the police. When they arrived, I yelled out, "My husband just got another woman pregnant, and now he won't leave. I don't want him in this house! Make him go!"

The cops asked Eddie to leave quietly. He reluctantly went downstairs, got in his car, and drove away.

Once the police left, I let go of the tears of anger and hurt. He had proven to me that I had been right not to trust anybody. An affair I could have tolerated—getting her pregnant put a whole different face on the relationship. I was devastated. Yet there was a small glint of satisfaction at having outwitted him with my detective skills.

The Detective

What a relief to be free of the worry of going to bed at night and also free of guilt for being the cause of Eddie's frustration and anger.

Eddie made several attempts to come back, and although part of me missed him badly, I realized that basically nothing had changed. Beside my sexual withdrawal, there was the huge difference between us in background, education, and interests. Not a strong basis for a marriage. The same thing might well happen again. Then what? I currently had a clear case of adultery, the only legal grounds for divorce in New York State in 1967. If I took Eddie back, that would be considered condoning his adultery. If he strayed again, I could not use adultery as grounds for divorce, since I had accepted it the first time. So, I decided to hire a lawyer to draw up a legal separation.

A few weeks later, I started dating a guy whom I really liked. We had a lot in common, and I had strong hopes for something permanent, but as long as I was married, he kept a certain distance. My lawyer, instead of getting Eddie to agree to a divorce, only antagonized him and couldn't get him to sign.

The situation dragged on for months. I was fed up. It was time to use my skills as a detective again.

The yellow cab made it easy to keep tabs on Eddie. I had managed to get a peek at Jackie's driver's license in the glove compartment of her parked car, so now I knew her last name and that she lived in Lynbrook, Long Island.

Eddie usually took weekends off, and one Sunday, I drove out to Lynbrook and had no problem spotting the yellow cab parked in front of a small apartment building on the main thoroughfare. One day, while Jackie was at work, I went into her building and found her name on the door of a second-floor apartment facing the street.

The following Saturday afternoon, when the cab was nowhere near Eddie's rooming house, I again drove to Lynbrook and parked on a side-street with a good view of the windows and the front door of Jackie's building. The yellow cab was nowhere in sight. I stayed in my car and kept my eyes glued on that building. I barely noticed a little girl riding her bike up and down the street. Finally, Eddie and Jackie came out of the building and drove off in her blue car. Now I knew for sure that he was with her. After a while they returned, carrying packages and dry-cleaning.

As I was muttering to myself, "How domestic," a young woman strode over to my car. "What are you doing in front of my house?" She said scowling. "I know you're watching my little girl. What do you want with her?"

"I'm very sorry if I worried you. It's not your little girl I'm watching, it's my husband. He's having an affair with the girl living in that apartment building on the corner, and I'm trying to catch them together."

"Oh, you poor dear. You can park in front of my house any time you need to. You must be thirsty. Would you like a cup of coffee?"

A few minutes later, I gratefully wolfed down the doughnut and coffee she brought out. Then she asked me, "Are you aware that the township of Lynbrook just passed a law that forbids street parking after 9:00 p.m.?"

I had not known that and wondered how I could watch the apartment that night. Then I noticed some still unfinished houses across the street and devised a plan. Eddie was totally predictable, and he liked to go to the movies on his night off. Sure enough, right after dinner at 7:30 p.m., he and Jackie emerged from her building and drove off in her car. I followed them, unnoticed, to the nearby mall, where the only movie was playing. I watched them park and then drove home to Howard Beach to prepare myself for the night. I knew the movie would last at least two hours. It took me only one hour to collect an old blanket, a flashlight, a shovel, a sweater, and a sandwich and get back to Lynbrook. I parked my car behind one of those unfinished houses and set out on foot to look for the cab. Where the hell was he keeping it at night? Jackie must have a garage for her car somewhere. A couple of blocks away, I spotted that bright yellow cab through the window of a two-car garage.

Satisfied, I hurried back to my observation spot. The sidewalk had been paved, but a deep ditch ran the length of the houses where the curb was to be built. With my little shovel I excavated a space long enough and deep enough for me to lie in and keep my head below street level. I put on my sweater, ate my sandwich, rolled myself in the blanket, and waited patiently. I was ensconced in my hiding place shortly after 10:00 p.m.

I knew Eddie and Jackie would have to drive past me to get to Jackie's garage and from there walk past me to get to her apartment.

There was hardly any traffic. Finally, at about eleven o'clock, a car passed by and shortly afterward I heard voices coming from the direction of her garage. As the voices got closer, I recognized Eddie's. I held my breath as their footsteps scraped on the sidewalk right above my head. When I dared to look up, the light in Jackie's apartment was on, but not for long. I relaxed a little and waited to see if Eddie left, but no one came out of that building. By five in the morning, I could safely assume that Eddie had spent the night with her.

I would have loved to have seen him coming out of the building the next day, but I had a dilemma: I was the soprano soloist in a church in Rye, New York, and was expected there for rehearsal at 9:00 a.m. I was very conscientious about my job, so I was forced to leave my post. Tired, stiff, cold, and hungry, I drove home, showered, and had a big breakfast. During my drive to Rye, I warmed up my voice and arrived ready to sing, "Onward Christian Soldiers, Onward as to War."

My lawyer had drawn up divorce papers, appropriately giving the cab to Eddie and the house to me. Eddie had agreed to the terms, but still refused to sign the papers. But now I had a weapon. A few nights later, I parked right in front of Eddie's boarding house. Not only was the cab parked there, but also Jackie's car. I had brought our dog Toby along, and the two of us waited in the car. When Eddie came out, he couldn't help but see Toby, who was jumping and barking with excitement. Eddie escorted Jackie to her car before he got into mine. He greeted the dog, then asked me, "What are you doing here?"

"I came to get you to sign the divorce papers."

"But I don't want a divorce. I love you and I want to come back. The problem with Jackie is resolved, and I'm not seeing her anymore. She only brought something I forgot in her apartment. This is the first time I have seen her in weeks."

"Unless you want Jackie dragged through the divorce court on an adultery charge, you'd better sign these papers."

"But Gisela, I'm not seeing her anymore."

"Oh sure. I know exactly what you are doing. For instance, last Saturday afternoon you went shopping with Jackie. Then she cooked dinner for you and the two of you went to Green Acres cinema. You got back at eleven, parked her car in the garage down the street where you keep your cab, and spent the night with her."

There was a long silence.

"All right, give me the papers, I'll sign."

Two months later I was a free woman.

Susie

My old boyfriend, George, had a younger sister, Susie. I had met the family a number of times, and her mother decided that I was the right person to accompany Susie on her second trip to Vienna. Her first trip she had been for psychiatric treatment. While she was there, she interviewed some entertainers for a Mexican magazine, but one of those interviews was a little too intimate, and she came home pregnant. The father was a popular singer at the time, but married. Years later, Susie read in a magazine that this singer was separated from his wife. She thought if he knew he had a three-year-old daughter, he might be inclined to marry her. Thus, in 1960, I was offered a free trip to Europe in return for chaperoning Susie on her mission to reconnect with the musician.

I decided to take that opportunity to see what I could find out about my birth mother. I hadn't known anything about her, until my father sat me down at the age of twenty-one and told me many negative stories about her. Apparently, she had been diagnosed with hysteria with a proclivity towards pathological lying. Several times, she had attempted suicide, and she had spent time in a mental institution. As I grew up, my father made sure to remind everyone that I was just like my mother, and shared her pathologic traits. I however didn't consider myself to be all that bad, and I imagined my mother wasn't either.

I realized that looking for information about her after all these years was probably a wild goose chase. There was no word from her for thirty-three years; on top of that, much of the Rhineland, where we had lived, was heavily bombed during the Second World War. So, I didn't expect to find out much in the way of records.

Düsseldorf, Germany, was to be the next to last stop of my trip. Before getting there, I planned to meet the lawyer in Cologne who was handling a restitution claim I'd filed against the German government. Susie planned to fly home from Cologne while I travelled to Düsseldorf and made inquiries about my mother. Afterword, I planned to take the ferry to England to visit my Aunt Gerda in Bournemouth.

Susie was loaded down with a large number of suitcases and tote bags, which made traveling by train or bus very cumbersome for us. A car would make traveling much easier. So, when we arrived in Vienna, I quickly bought a used Volkswagen. Now Susie and I could travel comfortably in Europe, and I would bring the vehicle back home to the United States.

There was only one problem, or rather two: first, I had never driven a standard shift before, and second, I wasn't familiar with European traffic signs. Shortly after picking up the car, I turned into a street only to be confronted by a policeman on horseback. He pointed to the one-way sign, which I had ignored, and motioned me to back out. Totally flustered, I tried to get the car into reverse, but each time I tried, it stalled. Given my pathetic appearance, the policeman finally took pity on me and let me drive forward to exit the street. Much relieved, I decided it was wise to practice using the clutch before continuing our journey.

We located the singer's address, and I rang the doorbell. He very politely informed me that he was back with his wife and had no interest in Susie or their daughter. Then he abruptly closed the door in my face. I thought it was best to make no further attempt at getting Susie married. We might as well enjoy the rest of the trip.

We had to visit Venice, of course. We parked the car in a lot outside the lagoon and registered at a nearby hotel. Once settled in, we took a motorboat to the Piazza San Marco and took lots of pictures of the pigeons. In the afternoon Susie wanted to go swimming. We went to the Lido, which borders the ocean, and enjoyed a lovely swim in the sunshine. Later, we ate dinner at one of the local hotels. Then we went "bumming." We ended up at a trattoria, where two nice young men danced with us and bought us drinks. Around 10:00 p.m., I noticed the first signs of a bladder infection. It must have been from swimming in that cold ocean water—it had happened to me once before after a day at Jones Beach. I had to excuse myself more frequently to go to the bathroom. With each visit, I could see that the amount of blood in my urine was increasing rapidly; this was serious. I needed antibiotics. Susie—in a fumbling hybrid of elementary Spanish and Italian—tried explaining to our new companions that we had an emergency. They were quick to understand. Taking immediate action, they hoisted one of us onto a Vespa, and the other onto a Lambretta. Off we went to the only hospital on the Lido. Piercing shocks of pain ran through me as the motorcycle bounced over the cobblestoned streets.

It took twenty minutes just to find someone to open the door—there was no emergency service like in the United States. Susie finally convinced the porter to let us inside. If only we knew the word for bladder in Italian! With "infeccione" and "mucho dolor," the doctor gave me a suppository for pain and a prescription for an antibiotic. Only one pharmacy was still open in Venice, and it was near the Piazza San Marco. We waited for the next motorboat: at night, they run on a limited schedule. The feeling of extreme urgency to pee was constant, and I decided to make a quick last trip to the bathroom, but it wasn't quick enough. As I squatted over a drain in the middle of the floor, I glanced out a small window overlooking the dock. To my dismay, I saw the motorboat pulling away. Susie was furiously waving and yelling, "La mia amica!" It was too late, the boat had disappeared into the distance, and I could only wait in agony for the next one.

When at last I arrived at San Marco, Susie was waiting for me. Excruciating pain was shooting through me and I was no longer able to walk. By some miracle, Susie found two men willing to help. Weaving their arms together, they made a seat for me and gently transported me to the pharmacy, where my prescription was filled. But when I used the bathroom there, I saw that I was now passing pure blood, and I was scared. I had never had an infection that badly. I needed to see a doctor. The office of the doctor on call was nearby, and the boys carried me there, then pleasantly went on their way. The doctor took one look at my urine specimen and gave me a shot of morphine for the pain. While waiting for the morphine to take effect, he made a strong martini for Susie. It was 4:00 a.m. by the time the doctor dismissed us. We had to take a taxi back to the hotel—in Venice that means a gondola, so we arrived at the hotel singing at the top of our lungs. I'm surprised the hotel let such crazy tourists back in. I had a high fever that forced me to stay in bed for the next three days. Susie explored Venice on her own.

After I recovered enough to continue with our trip, we spent a few days on the Riviera. Susie found another singer to interview. I tried to keep her out of his bed, but when he asked her if she would like to see some of his pictures, I could only urge her to be careful. I waited patiently with the man's secretary until the "interview" was over. Susie was difficult in other ways as well; she insisted on walking through the small town in her bathing suit, something punishable by law in Italy in those days.

Very early one morning we started out for Germany. Although Susie had a driver's license from her native Mexico, I had not yet trusted her with my car. But after driving several hours, fatigue set in, and reluctantly, I let Susie drive the next stretch of highway. I was taking a nap in the backseat, when I was awakened by a tremendous jolt. My little Volkswagen had collided with a large bus, which had suddenly loomed up in front of Susie as she was maneuvering a sharp turn. We got out of the car and saw that one side was badly dented and one tire totally demolished. The car would not start. A very handsome Frenchman—Phillipe—noticed the two damsels in distress and helped push the car to the shoulder. He also called a tow truck and stayed with us until it arrived, then drove us in his car to a hotel in nearby neighboring Bordeaux.

Meanwhile, Susie had contracted a vaginal inflammation and spent the night in a local hospital, whereas I spent a lovely evening with Philippe, which included a delicious dinner. He was a truly chivalrous Frenchman.

Susie's trauma over the collision, her vaginal problem, and the prospect of spending two more days in a hotel room while waiting for auto parts, convinced Susie that she'd had enough of the trip. She insisted that I should continue as planned. She managed to change her flight home to the very next day. Philippe and I saw her off at the airport and spent that day and the next night together.

Once my car was fixed, I said a sad goodbye to Philippe and drove on to Cologne. My lawyer turned out to be a pleasant gray-haired gentleman, quite paternal. He strongly advised me not to make inquiries about my mother. He was afraid that I would be deeply shocked by some of the unsavory facts he had uncovered about my parents while looking up court records in connection with my restitution claim. I thanked him for his concern, but of course, was now more curious than ever. I set out for Düsseldorf.

I lost touch with Susie, and sadly learned from her brother years later that she had committed suicide. I often wonder what happened to her daughter, but I lost contact with the family.

The Search for Mutti

I raced across the square hoping to beat the registry's closing time. A driver at the taxi stand had explained I probably could get information there. He added, "But hurry. All government offices in Germany close by one o'clock."

Just as I arrived, a woman was locking the front door. "Oh dear," I said, quite out of breath, "I'm from America, and I just arrived in Düsseldorf. I'm trying to get some information about my mother."

"Your mother! Do come in, liebe Frau."

The woman led me upstairs to a room with a microfilm viewer and there, looking under both Selo and Evers (my mother's maiden name). I found records of who was born, who died, who married, who divorced, who moved, and who emigrated.

My mother's current name was Heine, and both her husband and her mother—my maternal grandmother—had died within the past year. And what I had thought was a lonely child's fantasy, was real—I actually did have a little sister. Ingrid was four years younger, so we must have lived together for a year. She had stayed with my mother until right after the war, at which time she immigrated to England. A brother, Wolfgang, now just seventeen years old, was a total surprise.

The clerk kept herself busy while I studied the long microfilm. At the very end of the list of names and dates was an address. "Excuse me, this address—would you know how long ago my mother lived there?"

She glanced at the microfilm and said casually, "Your mother just moved there six weeks ago."

I took a deep breath. "She is still alive?"

"Yes, dear."

"And is living at this address?"

"Yes."

I thanked the woman for letting me stay after closing time and drove to the "pension" where I had planned to spend that night. I had to tell this incredible story to somebody. The landlady, almost as excited as I was, wrote down directions to the suburb Düsseldorf-Eller and wished me luck.

During the drive to Düsseldorf-Eller, I mulled over the situation. My mother was alive! I had never expected it. I had no mental image of her and no memory of the first five years of my life with her. My father had made sure that I had no visual reminders; he had cut out my mother's face from every photograph in his possession.

Now, here I was, on my way to meet the woman who was my mother. There were lots of questions buzzing around my head. What does she look like? Will I know her? Will she even remember me?

Those damned efficient Germans! A whole world war, almost total destruction of the industrial Rhineland, and here, thirty-three years later, was the address my mother had just moved to. My mother! The word "mother" had lost its meaning for me a long time ago. So I had no intentions of telling this stranger who I was, but how to explain my presence? I composed a phrase in German: *"Ich komme von einem Rechtsanwalt in Köln und möchte bitte ein paar Fragen stellen."* (I've come from a lawyer's office in Cologne and would like to ask you a few questions.) I memorized my speech while following the simple directions.

The house was a small suburban cottage with colorful flowerbeds all around. I managed to find a parking spot about two blocks away. As I was walking back to the house, I noticed a fancy red convertible with a British license plate among the small German cars.

There was no "Heine" on the front door. I walked to the back to look for another apartment and passed a big open window. Inside I could see a gray-haired woman, a movie-star-gorgeous blonde woman in short-shorts, and a bunch of small children. I assumed that this was some other family and continued walking towards the back. A suspicious "Ja?" Stopped me. In my fairly fluent German, I explained that I was looking for Mrs. Heine. "I'm Mrs. Heine," the gray-haired woman said. I looked at her and made a mental note: That's my mother.

I said that I would like to ask her some questions, and she motioned me back to the front door. We stood face to face. She was short and buxom, but nothing about her was the least bit familiar. I repeated my little speech: "I've come from a lawyer's office in Cologne and would like to ask you a few questions."

Very suspicious now, she said, "Ja."

"Did you ever have a daughter named Gisela?"

She looked at me intently for a minute, then stammered, "Gi- Gi- Gisela," and collapsed.

At the sound of her fall, the blonde woman came running out crying "Mutti!"

In a flash everything came together: a blonde girl, my sister now living in England, the fancy red convertible with the British license.

Trying to pick my mother up, the blonde asked, "What happened?" Then with a puzzled look she said, "Who are you?"

"Are you Ingrid?"

"Yes, who are you?"

"I'm Gisela."

"Gisela?!"

Together we got my mother off the floor and onto a chair in the kitchen. We were all talking at once, I was telling them how I found them. Ingrid was explaining that she was visiting Mutti with her two boys, as she often did during the summer. Mutti was telling the neighborhood children who had come to play to now go home. We were still talking, when footsteps sounded on the path outside. Mutti whispered, "Quick, hide in the bedroom, it's Wolfgang."

I hid in the bedroom, but left the door open a crack and listened. Mutti, all excited, said, "Wolfgang, you'll never guess who's here."

He shrugged his shoulders and mumbled, "I don't know."

"Gisela!"

Suddenly Wolfgang was all attention. *"Deine Gisela?"* Your Gisela, as if he thought Gisela had just been one of my mother's many fantasies.

Mutti nodded triumphantly.

I was touched. Wolfgang, who was born sixteen years after I had disappeared from my mother's life, thought of me as "her Gisela".

Just in case my mother needed a reminder of who I was, I had brought a photo of me at about age four. Half of the picture had been cut off. Mutti said, "I have that same photograph."

She found the picture. I had always assumed that the other half showed my mother's face, but no, it was a picture of my baby sister Ingrid with my hand on the cradle. On the back of her copy my mother had written, *"Werde ich je meine verschollene Gisela wieder finden?"* Will I ever find my lost Gisela again?"

I controlled my tears. All those years that I had felt abandoned and unloved, my mother had thought about me, talked about me, missed me, and tried to find me!

Gisela in New York City.

Gisela's great-grandmother, Lina Marx (née Kappel), 1862.

Three of Samuel and Alice Sara Selo's five children (from left to right): Richard (1896–1947), Hans (d. age three), and Marga (1888–1953).

The Selo family's department store, Düsseldorf, Germany. Founded by Gisela's "Grosspapa," Samuel Selo.

Gisela's Father, Herbert Selo, and her mother, Claire, on their wedding day.

The flat where Gisela was born on February 14, 1923, Krefeld, Germany.

Gisela with her parents, Claire Evers Selo and Herbert Selo, c. 1928.

A young Gisela enjoying the beach on holiday in Holland, c. 1928.

Herbert Selo, on his way to St. Louis, Missouri, 1951.

Herbert Selo, as an intern at Mt. Sinai Hospital, New York, 1939.

Gisela's father, Herbert Selo, 1898-1953.

Herbert Selo, Biochemical Institute of the Städtische Krankenanstalte,
September, 1920.

Alice Sara Selo with her daughter Margarate Klare Selo, Gisela's aunt Marga.

A Portrait of Alice Amalie Sara Selo (née Marx), Gisela's paternal grandmother. Affectionately known as "Grossmama."

*Portrait of Gisela's aunt
Gerda Selo.
Born January 23, 1900,
Germany.*

*Gerda Selo, England, 1930s.
Gerda fled Nazi Germany in
the 1930s and immigrated to
Bournemouth, England. Here,
she opened a successful dental
surgery.*

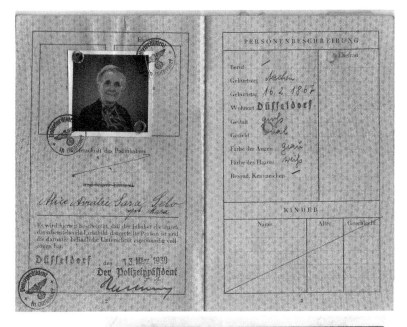

Above: Passport of Alice Amalie Selo.

Right: Alice Amalie Selo in England.

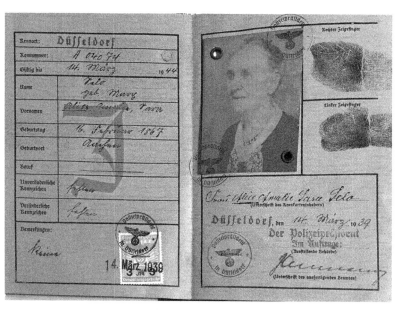

*Top: Passport of Marga Selo marking the day she and her mother left
Germany for England. Bottom: Passport of Alice Amalie Selo.*

Engagement photo of Alice Kapell and Herbert Selo, married August 6, 1930, Krefeld, Germany.

Wedding Announcement and menu marriage of Alice Kapell and Herbert Selo,

Speisenfolge
—
Verschiedene Vorspeisen
—
Bouillon in Tassen
—
Rheinsalm
—
Verschiedene Gemüse
Zunge und Pökelfleisch
—
Junge Hähnchen
Salate und Kompotts
—
Eis
—
Mokka und Gebäck
—
Abends: Kaltes Buffet

Gisela (third row from bottom, far left) in a class photo from her school in England.

High School Girl Tells Of Flight from Germany

MISS Ruth Selo, a junior in Findlay Senior high school, talked informally to the fifth period and Spanish classes, Tuesday, afternoon. Miss Selo, who was born in Germany and who came to Findlay only this summer, first told her life story and then answered questions asked by other students.

She explained that she, and later her family, fled from Germany into Holland shortly after the rise of Hitler into power. Later she went to England and attended a girls' boarding school. She came to America after much trouble getting permission to leave England because she was a German citizen. When she arrived in Findlay she saw her parents for the first time in two years.

When asked if she liked the American school system better than that of the English, Miss Selo replied that she did because here students are given a wide variety of subjects to choose from, whereas in England the choice is limited to a very few subjects and most of these are compulsory. She said the English are "much more formal than the Americans."

Miss Selo explained, in reply to a question asking what form of government she liked best, that she liked dictatorships least of all. She said the kingdoms, England and Holland, were very nice, but that in Holland her father, who is now a doctor in Findlay, was not allowed to practice because he had not lived there long enough.

Miss Selo said that even though the food is rationed in England, it is very plentiful. She explained that the English are very confident they will win the war.

The ambitions of Miss Selo are to write a book of her life and to become a foreign correspondent. She can speak Dutch, English, French, and, of course, German. She is now studying Spanish at the high school.

Newspaper clipping of article interview with Gisela just after her arrival in Findlay, OH.

Sencior portriat of Gisela Ruth Selo, Findlay, OH, 1942.

Gisela with her first husband Mike Sterngold, Ohio, summer, 1947.

Gisela and Mike,
Ohio, 1947..

Gisela with her stepmother, Alice, Findlay, Ohio 1939.

Eddie, Gisela's second hustband, in his twenties.

Gisela and Eddie in Howard Beach, NY, 1963.

Gisela's longtime partner, "Cosa Nostra Chris" enjoying a sunny day in Howard Beach, NY.

Chris caught diligently reviewing "the books" for Gisela's jewelry business.

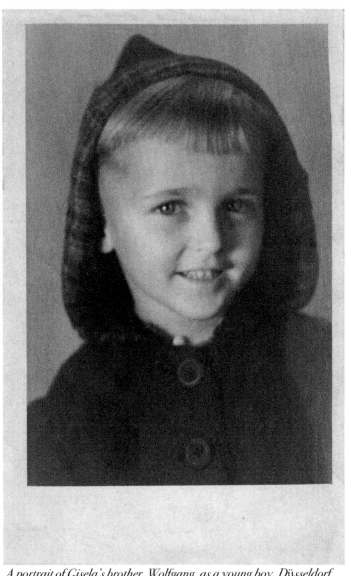

A portrait of Gisela's brother, Wolfgang, as a young boy, Düsseldorf, Germany, 1946.

Left: Gisela's mother, Claire Evers Selo, with her daughter Ingrid, and Ingrid's two sons, Anthony and Michael, England, 1972.

Below: Gisela dining with the family she found later in life: brother-in-law Joe, mother Claire, and half-sister Ingrid.

Top left: Wolfgang shortly before his untimely death.
Top right and above: Gisela with her half-sister Ingrid.

Gisela in costume clockwise from top: Gisela as Octavian in Struass' Rosenkaba-lier, Gisela in Verdi's La Dame aux Camelias, role unknown.

Above: Gisela dining with a mysteriously unnamed man featured in many of her photos.

Right: One of Gisela's many loves.

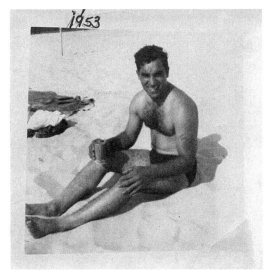

Left: An Italian boyfriend, Italian Riviera, 1953.

Below: Gisela and her first husband, Mike, at a formal event.

Fashionable Gisela outside her home in Howard Beach, 1971..

Gisela outside the Howard Beach home, 1971.

Gisela and Guy Frey enjoying a special night out at The Waldrof Astoria, New York City, 1962.

Gisela with-long-time friend, Guy Frey, New York City, 1950s.

*A pocket-size shot of one of Gisela's
many lovers, Hal Armbruster.*

Gisela in her mid-twenties, with a friend.

Gisela in costume.

Gisela in her later years.

Gisesla at The Hallmark after her 80th birthday.

Wolfgang

My half-brother was already seventeen, when I finally discovered my mother, Claire, alive in Germany. Although he was a tall, handsome kid, I saw signs of a very disturbed personality. At times, when my sister and I were visiting, he would disappear for days. When we asked him where he had been, his usual answer was *"Lass mich doch"* (leave me alone). In general, he was morose and taciturn and often hungover. But, I identified with this troubled boy. I understood his struggle to connect with people. We also bore a physical resemblance—we both looked like my mother.

Things were made worse by my mother: she made constant excuses for Wolfgang. With pride, she told us how she used to hide him under the bed when he would play hooky from school and the authorities came looking for him. She was always there to cover for him; he never had to take responsibility for anything. She would even finish his sentences for him. She never allowed him enough freedom to individuate. As a teen and young adult, he worked as a waiter in the evenings, and he frequently stayed out all night; Mutti would then let him sleep all the next day. Sometimes he came home wearing expensive gifts; we didn't dare ask where he had found them. I suspected he was prostituting himself. Always impeccably dressed, he had learned tailoring, but preferred waiting on tables.

Mutti later wrote me that he had married, and naturally my mother didn't approve of the bride. I believe she was jealous. Unused to sharing Wolfgang's attention, she paid little attention to his wife, and the baby girl born during the marriage. Wolfgang was never sure that the baby was his. After he was drafted, he heard rumors that his wife was running around with other men. When he went AWOL from his army regime and caught her in the act. They divorced and Wolfgang washed his hands of the entire unpleasant relationship. He told me that they were better off without him, anyway.

Wolfgang never did finish his military tour of duty, so he had no working papers and was forced to work off the books and without benefits. He was never secure, constantly looking over his shoulders, for the Germans were very strict about enforcing rules of military service.

Wolfgang also suffered a thrombosis in his leg and was unable to walk for a period of time. He lost all his teeth due to gum disease related to his poor nutrition and excessive drinking and smoking. Not long after, I heard that he had contracted tuberculosis and spent a year and a half in a sanatorium. He was discharged with strict orders not to work anywhere near food, so his days as a waiter ended.

My brother-in-law, Joe (Ingrid's husband), offered him a job in England, and he took it. Alas, one day without permission, he took Joe's Jaguar for a joy ride. Joe reported the car stolen, and Wolfgang was arrested. After this event, Joe sent him back to Düsseldorf, wanting nothing more to do with him. Ingrid would continue to see him and she did what she could to help him financially.

Wolfgang was born in 1945, just before the end of World War II, when conditions in Germany were horrendous. Mutti suffered from severe post-partum depression and refused to breast-feed her newest infant. Milk and formula were scarce, so he started life undernourished and neglected. Mutti told me that Wolfgang's father wanted to marry her, but she was afraid that he might take the boy away (echoes of my father's behavior). He was destined to remain illegitimate. Another strike against him.

When Mutti went to the hospital to give birth to Wolfgang, the baby's father tried to rape my fifteen-year-old sister, Ingrid. When Ingrid told Mutti, my mother dismissed the accusations without a moment's pause. Out of resentment, Ingrid had always considered Wolfgang a bad seed. I knew better, but I also knew he was troubled and needed help. After all, hadn't therapy kept me from total self-destruction?

On one of my visits to Düsseldorf, I convinced Ingrid that Wolfgang needed psychiatric help, but we were sure that he would refuse it. At my suggestion, we contacted the appropriate military authority, and after convincing the commanding officer that Wolfgang needed psychiatric treatment, he agreed to help, as long as Wolfgang was under his personal jurisdiction. We to let the officer know when Wolfgang was at home, so that he could be arrested.

The next morning, after Wolfgang came home, Ingrid went out to get fresh rolls and called the commanding officer. While we were eating breakfast, the military police came to arrest

Wolfgang. We tried to explain to Mutti that it was best for Wolfgang to finish his tour of duty, but she became hysterical. Ingrid and I went out for a while, and when we got back, we were totally dismayed to see Mutti sitting at the kitchen table talking to Wolfgang, as if nothing had happened. He told us proudly that he had runaway at the first opportunity. Ingrid and I said nothing. All our efforts had been in vain.

I found out later that Ingrid told Mutti I was the one who had instigated Wolfgang's arrest. Although Mutti never mentioned the incident to me, but I knew it was one more barrier between us. I never had the opportunity to explain my motives, and in Mutti's mind I was now just like my father, trying to take away her child.

One evening Wolfgang invited me to go with him and see the old city. I was delighted. We spent the evening bouncing from one bar to another in old Düsseldorf. He was greeted as an old friend in every bar we visited. The more beer I drank, the more I felt attracted to this handsome young man. The attraction was mutual. As we walked home at daybreak, we spent a lot of time kissing passionately. After all, we had not known each other as brother and sister until very recently. For a while, I felt strongly that I loved him, and we exchanged a number of love letters. I wanted to bring him to the States where I felt I could get help for him, but realized we had an impossible situation. I didn't have enough money to support him, and what would he do? His English was limited, and I didn't think he could fend for himself. Gradually we stopped corresponding.

A couple of months after my mother died, Wolfgang was sent to the hospital. He trashed the entire floor where he was being held, and the hospital had him arrested. I never learned the outcome, but a year later I received a letter from Ingrid with some shocking: Wolfgang had inoperable cancer of the esophagus and it was terminal. I decided that it was time to visit him and get to know him better before it was too late. He reserved a room for me and met me at the airport. Still handsome as ever, there were no obvious signs of illness. I was proud to walk down the street with him. I met him every day for brunch or lunch, and we spent a lot of time talking. He could no longer swallow solid food and lived on coffee, beer, Ensure, and cigarettes. We went to a nearby Zoo and took a boat trip on the Rhine. In the evenings I left him alone. I would have dinner somewhere, then head back to the hotel to read or watch TV.

One day, I mentioned that I still remembered "dicke Bohnen," a regional specialty. On my last night in Düsseldorf, he invited me to his apartment and prepared the dish for me. I felt truly honored; Ingrid had never been invited there.

When I walked into his apartment, I knew why nobody had ever seen it. It looked like a dumpster—parts of lamps, umbrellas, bicycles, radios, alarm clocks, and televisions were on every available surface. He would pick these items up from the street, fix them, then sell them at the bars whe frequented.

After he moved the bicycle wheel resting on his bed, we sat down. Although he was unable to eat anything himself, but he had cooked the beans with that special sauce exactly the way I remembered. He gave me the leftovers to take to Ingrid the next day. When I delivered them, she discarded them as if they were poison. I felt very hurt for him.

That was the last time I saw Wolfgang. I called him

regularly from New York, until one day I heard that he had thrown his phone at the telephone company's receptionist; he could no longer hear or speak. He died not long after that. Ingrid and Joe drove to Düsseldorf to take care of the funeral and discovered to their shock that his wife had already paid for the it. His wife! They discovered she owned a beauty parlor in Cologne. When Ingrid and Joe later met her, she turned out to be an older black woman from Guyana. As his widow, she had taken care of everything, and I was grateful. But, I must admit, I was still a bit shocked. When I had visited Wolfgang a few months earlier, there had been no trace of a woman in his apartment, nor any mention of a wife or marriage. I imagine their marriage had been a green-card opportunity with some financial arrangement.

I had gone to Düsseldorf to get to know Wolfgang better, but in the end, it seems I never knew him at all.

Depression

Today, a gray mist is hanging over everything. Nothing is worth doing; it all seems so pointless. I get out of bed in the morning, because breakfast is served between eight and nine, and I'm afraid that if I don't force myself to get up, I just might stay in bed all day. It's so tempting, but I do have to go to the bathroom, and the awful taste in my mouth needs rinsing out. Well, as long as I'm up, I might as well get dressed and go down to breakfast, I tell myself.

Now what do I do? With a heavy sigh, I realize that I didn't put away my clothes the night before—okay, my underwear goes in the hamper and my sweater needs folding, but it's too much effort to put it away in the drawer or to hang up my pants in the closet. I sit down in my recliner, pick up the weekly copy of the large-print New York Times and read the first article. I close my eyes and wonder; What did I just read? I haven't the faintest idea. I sit quietly for a minute. When I wake up forty-five minutes have passed. I tell myself: This won't do!

I go to the computer to do some writing, but first, I check my email. I delete any obvious spam, but I can't make sense of some of the messages. I close the email and open "Word."

I face the big blank page on the screen but can't find a single word to get me started. I decide that a game of Spider Solitaire is better than just doing nothing at all. I choose the easy version, but since I win almost every game, I select the next level of difficulty. I tell myself that I have to win three games in succession before I can quit playing. When I inadvertently look at the clock, I see it's 12:50 p.m.—time for lunch. Although I realize I will be late, I first finish the game I'm playing.

During mealtime, I behave quite normally. I don't think anyone notices that I'm not myself. I try not to show the overwhelming sadness inside me, and for a moment I get distracted by the innocuous conversation next to me.

After lunch, I make a shopping list, I really need a few things from the supermarket. But it's such an effort to walk the four blocks there and back. I'm just too tired. I'll go another day. I decide to vocalize, and try to put a performance program together. I pull my computer chair to the keyboard and play a chord. In despair, I bang on the keyboard, saying to myself, I can't, I just can't. I haven't the strength to sing. I haven't even the heart to sing. Why bother with this impossible struggle? Who cares anyway? I decide that nobody really cares and back I go to the computer for a few more games of Free Cell, before I resume Spider Solitaire, which requires much less concentration.

I knew that something was wrong when I found myself staring out of the Amtrak window on my way back to New York City, identifying with those small forlorn trees standing in the middle of the Hudson. They must have floated down river and taken root in the middle of nowhere. I was coming home after a family memorial for my cousin Ursula in Albany. Her son had told her story during his eulogy. I had not known how similar our early lives were. Born in the same town in Germany, both our parents divorced when we were three, and we were uprooted several times and as teenagers, including being sent to unwelcoming British boarding schools without knowing a word of English. Yet Ursula's life took such a different turn. She had found love and relationships in her life. More than three hundred people had attended her memorial service. Family and friends had come from Maine, California, and England. Who would come to my funeral?

By the time I got home, I was exhausted, and overwhelmed by sadness. During the next few weeks, spending hours sitting in my recliner, I tried to figure out why and where my life had taken such a different turn. Gradually it became clear. After her parents' divorce, Ursula's father moved away and disappeared from her life for good. She was able to develop a close relationship with her mother. My father had done the opposite. Instead of disappearing, he was always there, sure to remind me that I was not worth the trouble I was giving him, that I disturbed the peace in the house, that I was in the way and not behaving as family members should. From letters I read after his death, I began to see that my father had also complained about me to family and friends, always including the comment, "After all, what could one expect, she is just like her mother."

I understood now why I never felt welcome anywhere; thanks to my father, my mother's reputation preceded me wherever I went. I did make a number of unsuccessful attempts to change that preconception, but eventually I stopped trying, and spent my adult life living up to my father's negative expectations.

The sadness I was feeling now was grief for those wasted years, for not fully utilizing my intelligence, gifts, and education. True, after years of determination and persistence and with the help of a perceptive and patient psychotherapist, I did attain a degree of emotional balance. And some of these things had become clear during the years of therapy, but only on an intellectual level. Now I was actually experiencing rage and resentment for my father for depriving me as a child, for making me feel that I had no right to be and no right to be loved. I realized that I didn't feel loved or wanted, because my father had made sure that this would not happen, and for the first time in my life, I was allowing myself to feel anger for him. At the same time, I also felt the full emotional impact of those wasted and underutilized years.

Overwhelming as the feelings were, I realized that it was absolutely necessary for my further spiritual growth and inner healing to go through this period of mourning. I would not run away from it by taking an antidepressant. It was high time that I dealt with those deeply buried feelings of hurt and anger.

It took about three months before the sadness went away. One day, I actually felt like singing and arranged for a voice lesson again. I have since set up a painting schedule and was finally able to write this most recent chapter of my life. I feel more like my optimistic self, and although I still get periodic flare-ups of sadness, I am once again working to make up for those lost years.

Back to Singing

It was all Charlie's fault. Charlie was an eighty-year-old member of the Howard Beach Senior Center. Although he was getting senile, suffering from memory loss, hearing, and eyesight, everybody loved him. He was impeccably dressed in suit and tie, always smiling and cheerful, and kissed all the ladies' hands at every opportunity.

On Monday afternoons, an accompanist would come to the center and play for anybody who wanted to get up and sing. This included about six or seven people with varying degrees of ability. Charlie was always one of them, even though he knew only one song: "Nothing could be finer than to be in Carolina in the morning." Because he couldn't hear the piano, he was usually in a different key and always out of sync. Nor could he remember the lyrics either or decipher the words that someone had written out for him.

I had been coming to the Senior Center for more than six months. One Monday afternoon, the members were talking about the upcoming talent show. They were all planning to participate, including Charlie. I couldn't believe he would actually be permitted to perform, but apparently there is a law that a senior citizen cannot be denied any activity, as long as it is not harmful to anyone.

After my voice teacher at Juilliard had told me that she thought that I had no talent for singing, I had promised myself not to go through the frustration of trying to sing with my damaged vocal equipment. Usually, I just sat in the back of the community room and listened to the others. That afternoon when I got home, I literally knocked myself on the head and said, "Gisela, what is the matter with you? You graduated from Juilliard as a voice major. Here Charlie is, ready to perform, no experience or expertise, and you won't open your mouth!"

The very next day, I told the center's director that I wanted to sing in the talent show. She was skeptical and said, "You better check with the accompanist next Monday."

Having now made a definite commitment, I wondered what on earth I could sing for this audience—certainly not opera or lieder. I found my copy of "Summertime" by George Gershwin in my piano bench. I tried it out, and although a bit rusty, my voice seemed to work as it had twenty-three years before.

At the talent show, I was the belle of the ball. Boy, did I eat it up! One woman asked me if I were interested in joining the Miss Senior America competition. Suddenly, eager to show off my recently rediscovered voice, I auditioned. Not only was I accepted for the show, but I became one of the finalists. As a result of this performance in 2002, an acquaintance asked me if I would be interested in a voice teacher. She knew a woman in Queens who was very good. I jumped at the opportunity to have someone professional tell me how my voice actually sounded after all this time, and so an appointment was set up for me.

I rang the bell at an old-fashioned white clapboard house and had to wait quite a while before a woman opened the door. Once inside, I saw how the walls of the long staircase were covered with signed photographs of just about every singer whose name I had ever heard. Shown into the music room, I was introduced to Mrs. Marguerite Wolfe, a ninety-six-year-old lady. She was sitting at her grand piano, beautifully dressed, wearing hose, pumps, make-up, and jewelry. From the first piece I sang for her, she recognized that I had a problem with part of my voice. When I told her the story of the botched surgery and the resulting scar tissue, she started me on some very helpful exercises, which I practiced religiously at home. I eagerly awaited each lesson.

About three months after I started studying with Mrs. Wolfe, I received a phone call informing me that she had been moved to a nursing home near her son in Pennsylvania. I was devastated. I phoned her there at least once a week. She was terribly unhappy without her piano, but delighted to hear from me. With great interest she answered all my questions about technique, and I can still hear her encouraging words at the end of each conversation: "Don't ever stop singing with that beautiful voice of yours."

About six weeks after she moved, I called as usual, but instead of Mrs. Wolfe, I got the following recording: "This number has been disconnected; no further information is available." I had no other contact numbers for her and never found out what happened. I could only assume that she had passed away.

In 2004, at age eighty, I moved to a senior residence in Manhattan. One of the activities offered there was an art class. Although I had sketched a lot when I was young and had actually earned a living coloring and painting black-and-white photographs, I had never studied painting. I was absolutely thrilled when I sold my first four paintings, and especially gratified when I saw four more of my pictures hanging at a fundraising exhibition in the lobby of New York Downtown Hospital. At the opening reception, one of the doctors commented admiringly, "You should have an agent."

"I wish someone had told me that when I was trying to be a singer," I sighed wistfully.

The doctor continued, "Oh, you sing too!"

I figured a doctor would understand the surgeries I'd had and the resulting scar tissue, and so I told him my frustrating attempts at being a singer. He listened attentively and then went to get something from his office. He returned with Bruce Baumer's phone number, explaining, "This man may be able to help you; he is a voice teacher who knows all about the anatomy of voice production and vocal technique."

I thanked him profusely, because not only had he really listened to me and connected me with a fabulous voice teacher, but he bought two of my paintings at three hundred dollars each for the fundraiser!

Five years of working with Bruce Baumer resulted in great improvement in the fullness and control of my voice. When I asked my previous doctor about the obstruction in my throat, he dismissed it with, "There's nothing wrong with your throat; at your age you have no business singing anyway."

In spite of those words, I have sung a number of solos, and each time the performance is better. I am now working on developing a more popular repertoire and applying the new technique to every piece of music. It is a frustrating process, because even when I sing with excellent technique and precision, I am still challenged by the physical obstruction on one side. I want to get it right, because, when I am able to do what the music demands, I get a wonderful sense of accomplishment.

Mutti

Often, in quiet moments, I relive finding my mother that day in Düsseldorf-Eller. The image and visit playback—I'm staring at her in wonder. Is this really my mother? Do I look like her? I marvel at the short and buxom figure before me as she speaks.

During my stay, I witnessed her sociable personality. Especially after a glass of wine, she was utterly charming and flirted outrageously with any man around, naturally, like a child. She fussed and fluttered about, and yet I realized that she'd had the strength to survive World War II in the heavily bombed industrial Rhineland—a single mother with two children, very little money, and on top of that, one who had been married to a Jew.

No matter how hard I stared at Mutti, I found nothing familiar about her; yet I had lived with her for the first five years of my life. Where were the memories? Why didn't I feel a rush of warm feelings for this total but blood-related stranger? I could not fake such feelings, and so I remained my cold, unapproachable self. No wonder she preferred my sister, who was beautiful and warm and bought her fine things and expensive dinners.

When I unexpectedly showed up at my mother's house, while my sister Ingrid was visiting, I ended up staying for the night. Ingrid's two toddlers and their nanny went to a hotel. The three of us talked well into the night—too late for a hotel, so we shared the one single guest bed. I had always been squeamish about physical contact with a woman, so even though this stranger was my sister, I felt pretty uncomfortable. It turned out alright though. We just talked the rest of the night, getting to know each other. We marveled that we both liked tailored clothes, had nice legs, wore our hair short, and had both suffered brief first marriages.

A British soldier had got Ingrid out of Germany just after the war, but he turned out to be an anti-Semitic, abusive brute, and she divorced him. My first husband was not that bad, just a jerk.

Joe, Ingrid's second husband and the father of her two boys, was an Orthodox Jew. My mother had told Ingrid that we had the same father, so my sister had always thought of herself as half Jewish and thought it perfectly normal to have the boys bar mitzvahed.

Ingrid raved about her Joe. "He's such a wonderful guy, a terrific businessman, and now he's making a lot of money. When I married him, he had just a little shirt shop in the East End of London, and we lived in a rat-infested room behind the shop. These days, he's highly respected in business, and we have a great social life. He's also very generous, not only to his family and to me, but to Mutti as well."

Before I showed up, my sister had planned to drive to the

World's Fair "EXPO 58" in Brussels with my brother Wolfgang the next day. But Wolfgang had gone off somewhere that first night of my visit, we weren't sure he'd return. Luckily, he showed up the next morning with fresh rolls. My mother wasn't up to the two-hour drive to Brussels, but the three of us thought it was a fine way to spend the day. So late morning, we piled into Ingrid's convertible and headed-off.

At the border, the customs officer looked us over. "What is the purpose of your visit to Belgium?"

"We are going to the World's Fair."

He asked for our passports, ordered Ingrid to open the trunk, and then said, "You have passports from three different countries, and yet nobody has any luggage. What brings you together on this trip?"

"This is my brother and my sister," Ingrid answered proudly. "Hmm, three different surnames and three different nationalities! Please wait here."

He took our passports and disappeared into an inner office. After about twenty minutes, he reappeared and without saying another word, returned our passports and waved us on.

When we got to the fair, we bought sandwiches and sodas and sat down on the base of a huge column in the main hall and almost immediately fell asleep. We woke up at a quarter to five, almost closing time for much of the exhibition. Anyway, too tired to undertake the sightseeing now, we headed back to Düsseldorf.

I made sure to let my mother know that I would have much preferred staying with her than with my father. It wasn't until much later that I realized that by doing that, I had destroyed the fantasy she had built up about my wonderful "life with father".

Now she had to deal with guilt for letting me go. I also repeated some of the stories I had heard about her, and now regret that.

On my last morning, when I was alone with Mutti, I brought up my father's accusation about her denouncing him to the Nazis. She was visibly affected when she heard this and told me her side of the story. "Your father's father had been against our marriage from the start and would not allow Herbert or me, not even you, into the house. When your grandfather's death from lung cancer was imminent, your father begged me for a temporary divorce. He needed to show his father that we were no longer married, thus he would be allowed to go to his bedside. Of course, I readily agreed and let your father get the divorce without any dispute or financial settlement. He assured me that we would remarry as soon as it was decent. In the meantime, we met secretly in an inn outside of town, where we would not be seen." Self-consciously, she added, "We even spent several nights together. That's when I got pregnant with your sister. Your grandfather had not even died yet, when one morning I read the betrothal in the paper: "Last night, Dr. Herbert Selo and Miss Alice Keyzer, the nineteen-year-old daughter of a prominent Jewish businessman, announced their engagement at an elaborate party."

I stormed over to your father's office and confronted him with the notice. He laughed in my face. "Is it my fault, that you're such a stupid goose and believed all that nonsense I told you?" I was beside myself with hurt and anger, powerlessness, and destitution. At that moment I lashed out at your father with some terrible words. I can never tell you what I said." She looked away, overwhelmed with shame.

What could have been so terrible? It must have been

something like, "You dirty Jew!"

Whatever it was, in her heart, I think my mother believed that with those words she was somehow responsible for all that happened to the Jews in Germany.

It was time for me to leave and drive to Ostend, where I had booked a ticket for the car on the ferry to Dover. It had always been difficult for me to show physical affection to a woman; now it seemed quite natural to put my arms around my mother to say goodbye. She stood stiff as a board and did not respond at all. I turned away fast, so she wouldn't see the tears welling up in my eyes. I wept the entire 120 miles to Ostend and could not control the tears even while crossing the Channel. I pulled myself together just before I got to Bournemouth, where I was about to visit my Aunt Gerda.

I realized then that this cold parting by my mother, this stranger, whom I could not even remember, had an enormous impact on me. I visited Mutti several times and one year brought her over to the States for a visit. It was a disaster. Eddie and I had no social life, no friends. While we were working, there was no one for Mutti to talk to in Howard Beach. And too many times I had to say, "Sorry, Mutti, we can't afford that." The only thing she really enjoyed was the stage show at Radio City Music Hall.

Our relationship never improved. To my annoyance, Ingrid showed up every time I was alone with my mother. In not so subtle ways, Mutti made it very clear that she preferred Ingrid. While staying in my house, she asked Ingrid one night, "Would you like me to make you a hot chocolate before going to bed, dear?"

She did not ask me. And she constantly reminded me of the

wonderful things Ingrid and Joe did for her. After every visit, I would receive a long letter saying that she now understood me better and next time it would be different. But it never was.

When my mother was dying, I would not visit her in the hospital. I knew that my physical presence only brought her grief, and I left her alone with those who could comfort her. I called her every day as long as she could manage the phone, and I went to Düsseldorf for her funeral. On a dreary, rainy day her three children, with three different surnames and three different nationalities, were the only mourners walking behind the coffin. My mother had no friends.

I tried to explain to Wolfgang why I did not come while she was in the hospital. He sobbed, "And now she is gone."

"For me she was gone a long time ago." But is she really gone?

My Father

I picked up the phone. An unknown voice said, "Dr. Selo would like to speak to you."

Oh my God! The only Dr. Selo I knew had been dead for more than ten years. How could he have come back? "Dr. Selo"? I asked in a small trembling voice.

"Yes, Dr. Selo. Dr. Max Selo."

I heaved a sigh of relief. I had heard of Uncle Max. He was from the Berlin branch of the family—one of my grandfather's many brothers. He was old and coming to the States where his daughter lived. I arranged to pick him up at the airport and drive him to his daughter's house in Riverdale. I met him a couple more times after that before he died; in fact, during the subway strike of 1966, I walked the 134 blocks from 34th Street to Columbia Presbyterian at 168th Street to visit him. He told me a number of stories about my father. In fact, he had even met my mother and found her utterly charming. He was the only member of the Selo clan ever to say anything nice about her.

Uncle Max was the one who first told me about the

abtreibungen, for which my father had been arrested in 1931. It was not a word I had learned as a nine-year-old, and I looked it up when I got home. It meant abortions. My father—according to whom I could do nothing right, so, by logical deduction he could do nothing wrong—had performed illegal abortions! It was hard to digest.

Much later, I found out that the arrest was because of an illegal abortion he had performed on an Aryan woman who had regretted it afterwards and reported him to the German authorities. At that time he got away with paying a large fine and doing nominal jail time. I guess it pays to have an attorney for a brother.

It was also Uncle Max who mentioned the rumors about my father and his chauffeur. I don't remember the chauffeur at all, but I do remember when my father was brought in on a stretcher to the downstairs surgery. I had heard a great deal of commotion and run to the landing.

"It's the chauffeur," Anna, our housekeeper said, and gently led me back into the apartment. But it was too late—I had recognized my father's long fur coat, and I screamed, "Daddy, Daddy!"

Anna tried to calm me down. I yelled, "You lied. You sad it was the chauffeur."

Anna explained that the chauffeur had been killed and my father severely wounded by a huge truck tire that crashed through the windshield of their car, as they were driving on the highway.

While my father was laid up, an attractive, well-dressed lady often came to visit him. Shortly after he recovered from the accident, he got engaged to her. That's also when he took me from my mother, maybe because he needed me to complete the image of an ideal family, with father, mother, and child. It was the perfect cover in case there were any latent rumors in regard to the chauffeur.

My father, Herbert, or as most people knew him, Dr. Selo, was a man of medium height and build, with brown eyes and curly black hair that he kept under control with pomade. I inherited his heavy eyebrows and somewhat protruding eyes. His large ears and Semitic nose reminded me of Eddie Cantor, but without the humor. I could never figure out why women found him attractive. He married Alice in 1930. I was told to call her "Mutti," but she wasn't anything like my real Mutti. I don't think she was too happy either to be the mother of a six-year old-daughter when she was only nineteen.

When Hitler came into power in April of 1933, the Nazis used my father's old abortion case as a perfect example of Jewish moral decadence: a Jewish doctor destroying an Aryan baby against the mother's will. Luckily a colleague warned him that his arrest was imminent, and he and Alice fled with me to Amsterdam in the middle of the night. Not long after, although only thirty-four, my father had a major heart attack. He was laid up for several months. I was told repeatedly, "Be quiet, your father is very ill."

The early escape from Germany surely saved our lives, but my father never got over his anger and resentment of everything German. As a young soldier in Germany during World War I, he had been wounded and received the "Iron Cross" for bravery. Twenty years later he had to flee his country like a common criminal, leaving behind everything meaningful to his life: his standing in the community (he had recently bought the bürgermeister's (mayor's) palatial residence, complete with its elaborate furnishings), his chauffeur-driven Graham-Page, his medical practice with all the latest equipment, and whatever money and investments he possessed. Everything was gone.

Once he had settled in Findlay, Ohio, however, my father was once again highly respected as a doctor. He was willing to make house calls, something other doctors did not do. He also had a special talent for diagnosis. Doctors sometimes sent him patients when they didn't know what was wrong with them.

Within a year or so of settling in Findlay, my father had enough funds to buy a ranch-style house in a new development. Many of his patients were farmers and would pay him in corn or potatoes, so I wonder now if he went back to making money through his old sideline of helping pregnant women. I had no inkling of that kind of practice, in fact, when I got pregnant, my biggest fear was that my father would find out and do something terrible to me.

His letters to his sisters always showed that he felt sorry for me. "Poor Ruthie, she has so many problems." But he would never take any responsibility for being at the root of those problems.

When Alice divorced him after fifteen years, I stupidly thought he might need me, but in no time he married again. This time it was to Marjorie, the daughter of a Methodist minister with two teenage girls and a boy of nine from her previous marriage. I was not invited to the wedding.

I witnessed a lot of friction between the new couple when I came home for visits. During one argument, Marjorie slapped my father's face at the dinner table in front of me. Much as

I hated my father at the time, I could not bear to see him humiliated like that, but I didn't dare butt-in and just kept quiet.

Their Christmas card to me was from the Selo family, depicting the individual members: father, mother, two girls, and a boy (whose last name was not Selo). Even the dog was there, but no figure representing Gisela. I thought it was in bad taste to choose that genre of card, and worse, to send it to me.

After the funeral, Marjorie complained that my father was a morphine addict. I didn't believe her, but later my mother, who had lived with him in Germany thirty years earlier, told me a graphic story about his addiction to morphine. I had to accept it. I guess he had easy access as a physician.

Looking back over the eleven years I actually lived with my father, I realize that I didn't know him at all. I saw him as a cold and controlling disciplinarian, a strict father who was determined to squelch any sign of emotion in me. I rarely saw him smile, only when he listened on the radio to Jack Benny, or Fred Allen, or caroused with his two Scottie dogs. He smoked Lucky Strikes incessantly, and played poker once a week. I never knew him to go to the theater, concerts, or museums. During a flu epidemic in 1953, he literally worked himself to death. He knew his fragile heart would give out under that kind of pressure. I think he was tired of the struggle, and of whatever demons he had been fighting all of his life—He was just waiting for his heart to give out.

What an unhappy, tortured soul he must have been. None of his three marriages were successful and he considered his only child a complete failure. His work must have given him some satisfaction, although I suspect he still found it necessary to perform illegal abortions. I'm sorry he never got to know me or trust me; I might have been of some use to him. Might he even have loved me?

Old Howard Beach

As I mentioned before, when Eddie and I got married, he insisted we buy a house. I had been perfectly happy living in my large apartment on West End Avenue, but he couldn't see paying rent for forty years and at the end of our lives having nothing of value saved. At the time, taxicab medallion owners were required to live within the city limits. For weeks we checked out all the ads for two-family houses on waterfronts, but they all required down payments we couldn't afford.

Late one Sunday afternoon, as we were headed for the Rockaways, I noticed a wooden drawbridge operated by hand. Curious, we drove over the bridge to see where it went. Making left turns at each dead end brought us to an area of mostly run-down houses, where suddenly I spotted a "For Sale" sign in front of a brand-new, two-family house. When we walked to the back looking for an office, we saw that a canal ran directly past the house. Thrilled, we called the number listed and arranged to view the house the next day.

The upper story apartment had three bedrooms, overlooking Hawtree Creek, an inlet off Jamaica Bay. The price was $10,000 less than any other waterfront property we had looked at. I had enough for the down payment. We rented out the first-floor apartment. Within a month the mortgage was approved, and we moved in.

We were so delighted with the house itself, that it had not even occurred to us to check out the neighborhood. Old Howard Beach was originally a summer resort built around a luxury hotel far out on the water, reachable only by boat or by railroad. After the hotel burned down, enterprising fishermen-built shacks on stilts in that area, which was surrounded by water on three sides.

By the time we moved there, family houses had replaced almost all the shacks. The population consisted of mostly Irish and Italian construction workers with a penchant for fishing, boating, and drinking. Swimming was not permitted, but there was a motorboat club right across the canal from our house, and the activities over there were fascinating to watch. At the beginning and the end of the summer season, a big canon was fired, which made all the dogs in the neighborhood under beds or in closets. Besides fishing for flounder, many club members had to be fished out of the canal, as the pitchers of beer were refilled without limit. Everybody in the area had a boat of some sort, and a few homes still had outhouses instead of indoor plumbing.

As long as Eddie and I were together, we were too busy working to have much contact with the neighbors, but once we split up, I felt totally shunned. I think that the neighboring wives didn't want a reasonably attractive, unattached female around their husbands. Often I ended up feeling very lonely, watching my neighbors partying and barbecuing from my window, while I was working at my desk, coloring photographs.

Tenants came and went to my apartment. So did boyfriends, who occasionally pitched in with maintenance, but overall, I took care of the house and garden. I painted, even the ceilings, paneled a couple of walls, refinished the hardwood floors, and built wall-to-wall bookcases.

Without children, I had no reason to participate in school or church activities. As an aspiring opera singer, I had to vocalize, sometimes with the windows open, which caused the passing school children to yowl along, and the neighbors see me as a real weirdo. The final straw was that I occasionally had African American visitors: That made me totally suspect in the eyes of Old Howard Beach. I was dying to move back to Manhattan but picking up and delivering my work to various photographers required a car—Impossible to keep in Manhattan.

I was selling Amway products to supplement my income. I had introduced one of the products to the body shop where my car had been repaired. That's where I met Chris. He was one of the men hanging out by the shop as he kept racing pigeons on the roof its. He took a fancy to me and made the shop buy a lot of Amway products. Eventually, he asked me out to dinner. He was a totally fascinating man, and the fact that he was married didn't bother me at all, since he was not living with his wife.

One day, as I was driving by the shop, Chris stepped out in front of the car.

"Hey lady, where are you going?"

"I'm going to the hardware store to pick up some wallpaper."

"I know all about wallpaper," he said and got into my car.

He accompanied me to the store, then home, and the next day helped me hang the wallpaper. He continued to hang around and help me with various projects until his death twenty-three years later.

I had started a wholesale mail-order company, dealing in fine jewelry and was renting an office in nearby Jamaica. I had printed my own catalog and gradually built up the business. It meant going into the city every day to pick up the merchandise for that day's orders. My tenants downstairs moved out about the same time my office rent was raised, and I decided to make the downstairs apartment my office. I hired a girl from the neighborhood to take care of the phone, take orders, and do paperwork. I made sure she always got paid on time and when the business could afford it, I took a salary as the CEO and also paid myself rent as the landlady. I reinvested my profits into inventory, so I would not have to go into Manhattan as often, I also kept an eye towards eventually selling the business. Life now became a lot easier, but the move turned out to be a costly mistake.

One November day, the downstairs apartment was broken into. Almost all my gold inventory was stolen. I called the police, and the sergeant nosed around for a while, but didn't believe one word I told him. Not even when I printed out my $300,000 the inventory.

"I don't want to be made a fool of here," the policeman threatened, his face uncomfortably close to mine. By the time the crime team could be called in, whatever evidence there was, would have been destroyed. Twenty years of hard work and substantial savings for my retirement probably ended up in some junkie's pocket. I had planned to sell the business that year for $350,000, but now I was left with only "good will" to sell. In order to survive, I had to clear out the downstairs office and rent it out too pay monthly bills.

Chris

How I met Chris deserves more description, for he became an important part of my life. In order to avoid traffic when leaving Old Howard Beach, I would go out the back way, passing the south entrance to Aqueduct Race Track. I had noticed a body shop right across from the gate, and when I needed to have my car door repaired, I stopped there for an estimate. The owner, Bill, was a tall, good-looking guy, but an older fairly stocky man was the one that gave me the estimate—one I couldn't refuse, so I left the car to be fixed. Bill drove me home and about ten days later he and the other guy, Chris, brought the car back. Politely, I offered them a cup of coffee and they came upstairs. I had been flirting with Bill, but Chris was the one who did all the talking.

"How come a pretty lady like you doesn't have a husband to take care of her car?" He said.

"I'm divorced, so I have to take care of everything myself. I work as a photo colorist, but because I don't make enough, I'm also selling Amway products. By the way, we carry an excellent car wash."

"Well, bring some around and we'll try it out."

I stopped at the body shop the very next day and came away with a small order. A few days later, when I drove past the shop as usual, Chris stopped me and said, "Listen, that industrial cleaner you got removes all the oxidation from the cars. We tried it on one of the engines too and it works so well that customers are bringing in their cars for repair just to get them looking like new." This time Chris ordered a whole case and after that I got orders on a regular basis.

Besides helping me next with my wallpaper project, Chris also helped with the paneling I installed. Years later, it amused me to see that Chris's panels overlapped and were peeling, whereas mine were perfectly abutted.

Soon, I would stop at the shop for advice on other house projects like sanding the floor. Chris was always at there. He explained that Bill was a buddy from the Marine Corps who let him keep racing pigeons on the flat roof of the shop. In return, he was teaching Bill the ins and outs of operating a body shop at a profit: how to deal with the insurance adjusters, how to get new customers, how to collect from a delinquent client and generally how to make money. Bill had actually offered him a partnership, but Chris wouldn't take a penny. At night, he slept on a deck chair in a furnished room around the corner from the shop.

One afternoon Chris off-handedly asked me out to dinner. I wasn't even sure it was a real invitation, but just in case, I put on a nice dress and was ready at seven, but he never showed up. During the weeks that followed he totally avoided me. One day, when I saw him in the shop, I got out of the car and confronted him. "You act like you're mad at me. You haven't come out to talk to me for weeks."

"When I found out that you handed me a bill of goods—all this shit about being alone and needing help—when all the time you had a husband, I lost interest."

"Where did you get that idea? I've been divorced for over ten years. There's no husband in the picture, and I never lied to you about anything."

"What? I came to take you out to dinner in a chauffeured limousine but when I rang the bell, your husband answered, so I just took off. After that I didn't want to see you."

"I was waiting for you that night, but you never showed up."

"Yours is the only two-family house on 99th Street, right?"

"No, there's one at 161–27. I bet you went there."

We drove down 99th Street and sure enough, he had stopped at the wrong house.

After that he spent a lot of time at my house, especially since my bed was much softer than his deck chair. We seemed to complement each other. He advised me when I first started my mail- order jewelry company. We did argue about sending packages COD. He thought it was dangerous that the customer received the jewelry before I received the money. I listened to him, but it was because of COD shipping that the business really took off. Orders were going out every day. Chris would take the packages to the post office or the UPS, because daily pickups would have aroused suspicion in the neighborhood. Chris never allowed me to be personally affected by his "other "life. He never received a phone call at my house, although he was practically living there. He would drive to different phone booths outside the area to make calls.

When he had to go out of town, he always let me know

and unlike in past relationships, I never needed to ask him where he was going or why, nor did he ever volunteer that information. He told me early on that he was married, but had been separated from his wife for some years. I was surprised that his marriage didn't bother me, and it wasn't just because I wasn't interested in getting married again, but as I realize now, it was because I felt secure and loved.

During the months and years that followed, Chris told me many stories about his life, and I discovered who he really was. He was a member of the Cosa Nostra, no, not the Mafia. Those guys were Sicilian, and according to Chris, braggarts and show-offs like John Gatti and his gang. They turned on one another and could not to be trusted.

Chris's parents, both from the old country originally, had settled in Boston, but moved to New York City when Chris was quite young. He had been brought up to be protective of his sisters, so when some kid in school made an inappropriate remark about one of them, he went after him with an axe. After that incident he went into hiding on his great-uncle's farm in upstate New York. That's where he was really groomed. He and the other kids were taught to observe every detail about a person and his surroundings. He became an expert at reading body language and manner of dress and talk, so that nothing escaped him. He also told me that he had an extra chromosome, which enabled him to kill when necessary. (That was once the going theory but proven invalid long since.) Still, when his great-uncle needed one of the boys to kill a chicken, Chris was the first to volunteer.

In the Marine Corps, his reputation preceded him, as the

saying goes. He was made bodyguard to one of the generals and was always the last to leave a combat scene. He was the one whose job it was to see that no prisoners were left behind. Eventually, following those orders, brought him before Senator McCarthy of the House Committee on Un-American Activities. His trial resulted in a dishonorable discharge from the Marine Corps. Although his first name was actually Dante, he then took on his deceased twin brother's identity and became known as Chris or Junior. He joined union and waterfront activities, and when necessary hid out in his friend's basement or on his uncle's farm. It was there that he met his wife, Grace. She was a Native American, raised on the Mohawk Reservation nearby, a strict Catholic who did not believe in violence or divorce. One day, after they had been married for a while, Grace came home unexpectedly and found Chris, busy with mob cronies. She overheard some Cosa Nostra matters not meant for outside ears. She decided she could not live with such a man and moved out. Divorce was out of the question for her, but also for him. Once divorced, she could have testified against him and also about what she had overheard. Chris would have been expected to make sure that she remained silent forever.

"She is my wife and I wouldn't want to hurt her," he explained to me. "So we stay married, in fact, even now, we make sure we're seen together at weddings and funerals so that no one suspects we're not living together."

It was enough explanation for me. I was utterly fascinated by this man. I had never known anyone so strong and sure of himself and so innately secure. I realized from the very beginning of our relationship that Chris came from an entirely different society, one that had its own rules and regulations.

In this society he was respected as a loyal and honorable man.

One of my two dogs at the time was a black lab, whom I had rescued from the park. Sam was the most loyal and protective dog I had ever had. When it snowed, I used to let him run loose and later, as I watched him coming home down the block, he would let out a loud bark when he spotted another dog. The other dog would turn right around and run quickly away.

That's how Chris came across—with his powerful build and his low raspy voice. He naturally inspired fear in others. But, never in me. I always saw him as kind and helpful. He valued my intelligence and independence, qualities that often intimidated other men. I felt loved and appreciated.

Chris was so much man that he filled my life totally. After the initial passion subsided, we were just comfortable with each other. In the twenty-three years we were together, I never even looked at another man. The word "love" never passed between us, but in spite of my love-starved childhood, I never felt unloved with Chris. Once I asked him, "Why me?" His simple answer was, "You pleasure me."

One of Chris's younger brothers, Freddie, lived in Virginia. Chris had called a meeting with some of the members of the New York families and asked his brother to attend. On the day of the meeting, Chris arrived hour before the "sit-down" was scheduled. As he drove into the cul-de-sac where the gathering was to be held, Chris was immediately suspicious—he was early, but there were already several men loitering outside the building and a number of unmarked parked cars. He drove right out of the cul-de-sac and skipped the meeting.

As it turned out, Freddie had turned informer. The "sit-down" was busted and there was a massive arrest—this was the arrest that made District Attorney Rudy Giuliani famous in 1976. Chris could not understand his brother's betrayal. I told him that it might have been jealousy. Freddie had always been overlooked in the organization, because his great-uncle had never trusted him.

Chris, because of his powers of observation, was the only one who was not arrested. This was suspect in the eyes of his "family." That wasn't all; Chris and Freddie bore a strong resemblance to each other, so that Chris could no longer go out safely. He now always wore a visored cap and dark glasses. Whenever we were out in public, where he might be spotted, his first words were, "Let's get out of here." There were a number of guys, like Gatti and his Mafia cronies, who lived on the other side of Howard Beach, who would have been very glad if Chris were out of the way. Besides, in Chris's society it is automatically assumed "like father like son, like brother like brother." So he was in danger for several reasons.

Not long after the big arrest, Chris had a heart attack, requiring a triple by-pass. I was seldom home, driving to Brooklyn and Long Island to pick up and deliver photographs. I thought Chris would be better off recuperating at his sister's on Long Island, especially since she had been a nurse. Since his family knew nothing about me, Chris and I only communicated by phone, but a couple of months after his surgery, I drove out to meet him in a neighborhood coffee shop. He was barely recognizable; he was so thin and undernourished. He had refused to eat what his sister prepared for him. She kept insisting that she knew best, and as he tended to do with women, he stopped arguing with her. Consequently, the dog under the table kept getting fatter while Chris got thinner. I couldn't bear to see him like that, a shadow of his old self. I decided that we would manage somehow, and Chris came home with me.

I spent the next few weeks pouring over recipes and studying labels at the supermarket, until I became an expert at preparing food that followed his dietary recommendations and tasted delicious. Gradually, he regained his strength and eventually went about his business as before.

He had gone out of town many times during our time together, but this next time he was gone more than two weeks. I became worried, not only about him, but also because we had arranged for him to pick me up after my cataract surgery. Finally he called. He had driven Upstate and learned that his wife was in a hospital in New Hampshire. She was initially admitted to the hospital for pneumonia, but while there, the doctors had discovered something more serious, ovarian cancer. He was staying in her house in Vermont and driving back and forth to New Hampshire every day to sit with her. He did come back to pick me up after my cataract surgery, but drove right back to the New Hampshire hospital.

A couple of weeks later he returned, Grace had died. And there was more shocking news: Chris was financially destitute. It was customary in his society that when one married, all assets be put into the wife's name and this is just what Chris had done many years before. Grace had exclusive control of their finances and unbeknownst to Chris, she had spent every penny of their resources. The only thing left was a box of valuable coins that Grace had collected. There was no one to take care of her affairs, so Chris drove to Vermont several times to take care of things. He packed all her belongings in boxes and at my suggestion brought them to my house, so we could go through them together. Had I realized that there were 75 boxes in all; I might not have suggested that. As it was, we put boxes wherever there was a space, in the six rooms downstairs, on the stairway and all over my upstairs apartment.

Chris was not the same with me after his wife died. I suspect that he never stopped loving her and would have gone back to her, had she been willing. A pretty upsetting thought. He had started smoking again, which aggravated his emphysema and brought on another heart attack. I had driven him to the VA hospital in Brooklyn several times, but as soon as he felt a little better, he would discharge himself AMA (against medical advice).

He was not able to lift anything and so it was up to me to bring all the stuff that had accumulated in the office, upstairs. The downstairs apartment needed to be renovated and rented out again. The endless trek up and down the stairs, carrying box after box, affected my back so badly that I was in constant pain and ha to use a cane.

When he was home, Chris would fall asleep on the living room couch in his underwear and only get up for meals and to take out the dog. On nice days he would stay out with Toby for hours, He also became friendly with Mike across the street, who was forever sitting on his front stoop.

Mike showed an interest in the downstairs apartment and came over to see it. We arranged that he and his family would move in as soon as the renovation was complete. Chris tried to do some painting, but he couldn't even get up on the ladder. I hired a couple of guys, but Chris was so critical of everything they did, that they just walked out. I got somebody else and I maxed out my credit cards to pay for all this. Chris turned his monthly pension check over to me and somehow I got by.

The coins that Grace had been collecting were made of 14K gold and sterling silver.

Chris would take them out periodically and fondle them. He loved handling money --- oh no, not spending it, just counting it.*

The summer was over and it was getting colder. The months dragged on. Chris had become incontinent and although he would clean up after himself, he was dead weight as he slept there on my couch in his underwear, Toby at his feet.

He was barely civil to me now. I was suffering from high blood pressure, diabetes, arthritis, and spinal stenosis. With all those problems, I just couldn't handle Chris any more. I told him he needed to make some other living arrangements, maybe in a veterans' facility.

On New Year's Day 2001, he took the box of coins and went to visit his nephew John on Long Island. He came back at about 9 p.m. and told me everything was settled. He had turned over the gold coins to John, who had found him a furnished room in the neighborhood and Chris could take his meals with John and his family. There was even a nearby lot where he could keep pigeons. I was incredibly relieved. He still had his car and so we would be able to spend time together, but the burden of Chris's care would no longer be on my shoulders. I was glad he was there now to help me. The thermostat had stopped working earlier and the house was very cold. Chris went down to the foyer and into the boiler room, to see what was wrong. A few minutes later he called upstairs, "You had better take me to the hospital."

I grabbed his coat and helped him out to the car. He said,

"Take me to Northport."

"Chris, it's much too far and I don't know my way in the dark."

"All right, take me to the one in Manhattan." He'd had his bypass surgery there. As I was about to enter the parkway he said weakly:

"You'd better just take me to Brooklyn."

It was past midnight now and there was hardly any traffic on the Belt Parkway. I drove like it was the midnight ride of Paul Revere. Chris was leaning back against the seat, his eyes closed. When I got to the emergency entrance, I ran in. The nurse remembered me from my previous trips there. She got a wheelchair.

"No, no" I said, "this time you need a stretcher."

Together with an attendant, Chris was lifted onto a stretcher, dead weight and seemingly lifeless. I went along into the emergency room and as I watched a doctor bending over him, there was a sudden mad scurrying around his bed. A nurse sent me out to the waiting area. I surmised that Chris had gone into cardiac arrest.

It was five o'clock in the morning when finally I saw him being wheeled up to the ICU. I was allowed to go and see him, but he was not conscious.

"Come back tomorrow." Someone said.

I drove home, took care of Toby and headed back to the hospital about 11am. Chris was awake, but couldn't talk or eat. I asked him if he wanted me to notify anybody, but he shook his head, secretive as ever. I drove back and forth to that hospital for the next few days; he seemed to revive somewhat and gave me instructions, "If anything happens to me, call Patrick; he'll know what to do."

Patrick was the son of an old friend of Chris's and I contacted him that same day. I also called his nephew John, but John didn't visit him even once.

One morning the hospital called to tell me that Chris had been transferred to a nursing home in Coney Island.

My Chris, so strong and so vital, at the mercy of nurses and aides. It was hard to take. In a cheerful, sunny room overlooking the ocean, Chris lay, helpless. I offered to bring Toby out to the boardwalk where he could see him, but he shook his head. I turned away, so he wouldn't see my tears. He loved Toby; they had spent hours in the park together and for months Toby had been curled up at his feet.

I went to see him for the next three days; he slept the whole time I was there nor would he eat anything. It would have been better had they not revived him when his heart gave out on New Year's Day. Everything that was Chris was gone anyway.

On the fourth morning the nursing home called to tell me he was in the emergency room at Coney Island Hospital. I rushed over there; he lay in an overcrowded room with a tube down his throat, in spite of the DNR notice on his chart. When I complained to the doctor, she said "Do you want me to pull it out?" Could I say "yes?" Chris tried to say something, but the tube was in the way. He waved his hand in disgust and sank back into sleep. That night he died and I never got to say goodbye.

Patrick made the funeral arrangements. He and I rode alone behind the hearse; a long silent trip to Calgary, the military cemetery near Riverhead, way out on Long Island. Chris's nephew John and his wife met us there; a next-of-kin was needed to sign for the plot.

Grace had lived with John and his family for more than two years and had paid for both their daughters' weddings. One of Grace's boxes had contained nothing except loving notes and greeting cards from those girls to their aunt Grace. I asked John if they would like some of Grace's belongings.

"Just throw them in the garbage" was the hurtful answer.

Since I was completely broke, Patrick had laid out the money for the funeral. I asked John if he would please reimburse Patrick and mentioned the box of gold coins. John denied that there was anything of value in that box, and to Patrick said, "Why did you bother"?

"I couldn't let him be buried in Potter's Field," Patrick said.

"Why not"? was John's shocking answer.

"I guess you'll have to cancel the room for Chris," I said to John after the service.

"What room are you talking about?"

Apparently, John knew nothing about a room. As I write this, I keep wondering what Chris had in mind when he told me he had made other living arrangements.

I now took Toby to the park. A bunch of men recognized the dog and asked about Chris. When I told them he had passed away, they expressed their sympathy and added, "We will miss him and so will the pigeons; he was always surrounded by a huge flock. They gathered around his bench as soon as they saw the car."

When they told me how Chris had bought hot dogs and ice cream cones for himself and for Toby, I shook my head and sighed. Here I had struggled to prepare all the right foods for him, and a couple of hot dogs and some ice cream would have been much more appreciated.

I often feel guilty about asking Chris to leave when he was so ill, but I really had no choice. Still, that guilt will probably remain with me till the end of my days. John didn't want the flag draped over Chris's coffin. It now stands in a glass case on my bookcase. It has a plaque with the name of a man whom I knew to be loving and supportive and a man of honor.

Old Friends

I was born in Krefeld, Germany and lived there for the first nine years of my life. I had only two friends in my childhood that I remember and I met both of them in the same way: After school I used to go to my grandparents' house and it so happened that in both countries, a family with a daughter about my age, lived across the street.

In Krefeld my friend's name was Lore. She was one year older than I was and we played together after school for about two years.

Once we fled to Holland, there was no further contact with Lore or her family. I think I only remember her so well, because I still have the photograph of the two of us being hosed down in my backyard.

In Amsterdam my playmate across the street was Gabi, who became a really close friend during the 5 years we lived in Holland. Gabi and I spent our afternoons together, writing and performing plays for anybody who would listen. On dreary days we would spend our time drawing and painting. We invited our parents to our very original concerts; we would stand behind the drapes and twang our noses in close harmony and were sure that we sounded exactly like two guitars! Sometimes Gabi's other friend from the neighborhood, the now famous Anne Frank would join us at our very fancy tea parties. One of our fun activities was walking down the street together and loudly saying "Oh yes" to each other, thinking we would impress the passers- by with our knowledge of English! Little did we know then, that a few years later, English would become our primary language!

In 1938 I was sent to England. Gabi and her family moved to France, and when the Germans became a threat there, they also immigrated to the States. Gabi's father, who had been a wealthy banker in Germany, was now running a chicken farm somewhere in New York State. I think our fathers had a fall-out over money and for years there was no contact between them at all. Years later I heard that Gabi had run off and got married and was living in New York City.

Of Lore's family we heard nothing. I made some inquiries in later years, but I couldn't get any information and I assumed that the family had not escaped Germany in time and had perished.

The summer after graduating from the University of Michigan, I spent in Woodstock, IL at a seminar for foreign students. Before moving to New York City to live, my boyfriend, Johnny Walker, invited me to spend a week with him and his parents at their summer home in Vermont. They had a lovely house in the woods and welcomed me warmly as Johnny's girlfriend.

Looking back I realize I was in a very troubled emotional state at that point of my life and was not in the least aware that my behavior had any impact on other people. Instead of making my visit pleasant for everyone, I did my own thing. I had borrowed *The Fountainhead* from their library and stayed up all night, finishing it. Then I slept most of the following day; when I finally woke up sometime after lunch, I was still taken with the book and not in the mood to talk. I grabbed something from the kitchen and then took my dog Rusty, who had been with me all through the summer, for a long solitary walk in the woods. Not exactly an ideal houseguest!

After three days of my antisocial behavior, Johnny was totally disgusted with me and decided to drive home to New Jersey. I convinced him to at least drop me off in New York City instead of just taking me to the local bus depot. For five long hours he drove without saying one word and then he dumped me unceremoniously in front of the Pennsylvania Hotel with Rusty and my suitcase.

I knew nothing about New York City at that time and was certainly not aware that the American Legion Convention was in town for the weekend. That meant that there was not a room to be had, not even at the Y.

At a loss, I called my aunt and uncle in Forest Hills, but to my surprise my father answered the phone. He had come to New York because his brother was very ill and he said that he had no time to bother with me. I assured him that I only called to say hello and wasn't going to be a bother. So there was no help there. I was stranded in the middle of a strange city with my dog and my suitcase and hardly any money. In desperation, I called one of the girls who had also attended the summer program in Illinois. Her brother answered the phone and told me she hadn't come home yet. When I explained my dilemma, he invited me for the week-end and added that there was plenty of room in the apartment, since his parents were away as well. He gave me the address and since I couldn't take a bus with my dog, he offered to pay the cab fare when I got there. I was really grateful and didn't want to take any further advantage, so I spent most of the week-end looking at the ads in the New York Times. The nights we spent together.

First thing on Monday morning I answered a couple of ads and landed an interview that same day at Stouffer's on 57th Street. Next, I managed to find a room somewhere in Queens for just $10 a week, including breakfast and dinner. By Monday afternoon I had both a job and a place to stay. For $10 a week I was certainly prepared to share a room, but the landlady had neglected to mention that I would have to share the bed as well. In those days I was usually quite willing to share my bed with a guy, but I was most squeamish about physical contact with a girl. For fear of rolling over against the other body in the bed, I didn't dare close my eyes all night!

Exhausted from lack of sleep and the long commute from Glendale, Queens to 57th Street in Manhattan, I knew I had to find some other place to stay. I remembered my old friend Gabi who was supposed to be living in New York City. Through her parents I got her phone number and I was in luck once more; Gabi and her husband were in the process of moving from their single room in a residence hotel and thought I could probably rent the room they were vacating. That's just how it worked out and I became the proud occupant of a tiny room in a residence hotel on West 113th Street, between Broadway and Riverside Drive. Gabi and I resumed our friendship as if we had not been out of touch for ten years. I loved my new neighborhood and

Riverside Drive was the perfect place to walk Rusty.

The neurologist at the University of Michigan, had advised me to get psychiatric help when I got to New York. I suffered from severe headaches and never could understand or predict my own impulsive behavior. Gabi was working for the William Alanson White Institute of Psychiatry and she brought me back an application. I was eventually accepted for treatment and that's how my years of psychotherapy began.

After a few months Gabi and her husband moved to a larger apartment on 111th Street and eventually I also found a bigger place, a four room apartment in the basement of the building next door for just $45 a month. Gabi and I saw a lot of each other then, although I was careful not to intrude on her married life. She was petite, beautiful, intelligent and very elegant. Her apartment looked like a decorator's dream. A few months after their move, she got pregnant. Everybody was all excited and I helped as much as I could with the shopping and preparations for the new baby.

In her eighth month, Gabi had a miscarriage and was totally devastated; I wasn't very good at comforting people, but at least I was able to spend time with her in the hospital. The second day I came for a visit, the other bed in the room was occupied by a girl who had just had a baby. Her bed was surrounded by family and friends, talking and laughing and there were flowers everywhere. I paid no attention to the other girl; I was annoyed with the fact that she and her guests seemed totally insensitive to the fact that Gabi had just lost her baby. After some of her visitors left, I nodded a brief hello to the other girl. Her face seemed somehow familiar, but I couldn't place her. Her rather wide mouth reminded me of Lore, my old playmate from Germany. There was no sign of recognition on her part and I listened carefully for a German accent, but all of her visitors spoke like native New Yorkers. Gabi only knew her as Mrs. Davidoff, so I dismissed the whole thing from my mind. When I visited Gabi a couple of days later, Mrs. Davidoff and her baby had been discharged.

I couldn't get that face out of my mind. I told myself that it would be impossible to recognize someone after 20 years, especially when the last time you saw her she was just 10 years old. Gabi told me that she would gladly get that address for me; it would be easy since both girls had the same doctor. A few days later I got the address. Although I felt a bit foolish, I sent a note to Mrs. Davidoff, included my phone number and wrote, "If this name means anything to you, please call me," and signed it Gisela Selo.

Two days later I got a phone call and it was indeed Lore, my childhood friend from Krefeld! It was unbelievable that with all the hospitals in New York City and the hundreds of rooms in each hospital, my two childhood friends, one from Germany and one from Holland, should end up in the same room in the same hospital!

After our phone conversation, I visited Lore in Kew Gardens and we filled in some of the gaps of the past 20 years. I got to know her husband and of course, the baby. We met several times, but never got close; we had very little in common. Lore led the life of a Jewish housewife and mother, and I that of an aspiring opera singer, with no family obligations. Lore and her husband have since passed away, but I'm still in touch with her son Roger, the baby whose birth was being celebrated in that hospital room at Mount Sinai in New York City in 1952.

Gabi's story didn't end there. By the time we got together again, she was divorced and was raising her 2 boys alone. She had invested the money from her divorce settlement in an old landmark building in the West Village. She was in the process of total remodeling, knocking out a second floor to make high vaulted ceilings, tall stained-glass windows and converting one wall into a huge wood burning fireplace. She had a steady boyfriend and told me that she was now in therapy too. I wondered about her therapist, because some of her rather unorthodox ideas about raising her boys and treatment of her male basset hound quite disturbed me. I decided to keep my distance after that, but we did keep in touch by phone.

One day, years later, I received a letter from Wallkill, NY. Her father had passed away, but had sold the chicken farm shortly before he died, despite the fact that she wanted it. Now she was determined to get that chicken farm anyway. In order to have the money to do so, she had sold all her possessions including that landmark house in the Village and was finally living on that chicken farm in Wallkill, New York.

Several years later Marylou, another cousin of mine, asked me to join her and some friends for a weekend adventure at Lake Mohonk. Chris, my boyfriend at the time, drove us up on Friday and agreed to pick us up again on Sunday. Checking the map for the best way to drive back, I noticed that Wallkill was not far from the main road and I had the bright idea of stopping to say hello to my old friend Gabi. Before we left Mohonk I called her to get specific directions. She kept making excuses why we shouldn't stop by, but I wouldn't take no for an answer. Her directions were very vague, but I figured we would ask when we got to the area. Nobody seemed to know exactly find where she was using her address. We drove around for over an hour and finally found someone who at least knew who she was and gave us directions.

A turn onto a dirt road brought us to the correct mailbox. Just as we started up the hill, a small woman in dingy white shorts, her legs caked with mud came walking toward us in her bare feet. With her short pigtails and missing front tooth, I was barely able to recognize Gabi. She motioned us further up the dirt road to show us the chicken coops. There was not a cluck to be heard or a chicken in sight. She claimed she was having the coops remodeled. Then she led us past the farmhouse to an old grist mill with a small waterfall. She told us that this was her favorite spot and she would sit on that little wall and just watch the water. This was confirmed by a huge pile of cigarette butts on the ground by the wall. The next stop of the tour was the kitchen. It was a shock! There were dirty dishes everywhere, in the sink, on the counter, on the table and on each of the four chairs. It was difficult to move around, because even the floor was covered with dirty dishes.

Gabi offered us some fresh strawberries, which she had traded for some of the herbs she grew, but with the excuse that it was late already, we declined. We did need to use the bathroom, however. That was upstairs. My cousin and I groped our way through a living room with no working light. Vague shapes of big plastic bags stuffed full were everywhere. Before we got halfway upstairs we turned back holding our noses; the smell coming from a toilet that obviously hadn't been flushed for weeks, was unbearable. We got out of that house as fast as possible, As Gabi walked us to the car I asked about her boyfriend. She said he had to go to California, but would be back in the fall. In answer to my questions about her sons, she told me that they pitched a tent on the lawn when they visited, but she didn't seem to know when that was. We said a hasty goodbye. I told the others waiting in the car not even to get out. We would make a pit stop at the nearest gas station.

As we drove away, the tears were streaming down my face. What had happened to my intelligent, beautiful, elegant friend Gabi? To what extreme had her obsession and the anger at her father brought her? How could she end up like this after so many years of therapy? How could her sons allow her to live this way? I called her shortly after returning to the city and she said cheerfully that everything was great, her boyfriend was back and things were back to normal. I just couldn't believe her, but I decided that it was not my place to take on this tremendous responsibility and after that I only sent her a card now and then. A couple of times I received an unintelligible postcard covered with colored crayons with no signature or return address, but postmarked Wallkill, New York.

The last I heard from Gabi was when the envelope containing my 2008 Christmas card to her was returned unopened. On the envelope was printed: Moved: No Forwarding Address.

Eddie Encore

I had almost completely put him out of my mind, when one day, while cleaning out an old desk drawer, I came across his birth certificate and some photographs of his family. It didn't seem right to just throw them in the garbage, so I called him. I was greeted by Jackie's voice on the answering machine, asking to leave a message. A few minutes later, Eddie returned my call and still sounding angry, said he had no interest in the papers or the photos—just throw them out. Okay, I thought, that's that and forgot about it.

The very next day Eddie called back and said that he would like to see the photos after all. We set a time for him to come the following afternoon. I must admit I was curious to see him after 35 years. When I returned from lunch at the Senior Center, a man was getting out of a green jeep in front of the house. It had to be Eddie, but had I run into him on the street, I would not have recognized him. The past thirty-five years had served him well: he was still very attractive, with graying hair, a deep tan and a very muscular build. He had become a chauffeur, driving for a limousine company and was very proud of the fact that Paul Newman and his wife often requested him to be their driver, especially on long trips. From listening to his passengers, he had corrected his grammar and expanded his vocabulary. This had given Eddie new confidence and he was much more articulate than he had ever been. He was no longer the shy, hesitant kid from the Bronx; he had become a man, self- assured and confident.

There was now no trace of the old hostility as we talked over a cup of tea. In fact, he was kind and quite understanding when I explained that my sexual problem was caused by my deep-seated fear of commitment. He even asked me if I needed money, (I didn't then). I told him that the house was up for sale and that I had reserved an apartment at the Hallmark in Manhattan. For two hours we talked like old friends. Just before leaving, he called his wife to let her know that he was on his way home. I walked him down to the front door and as I said goodbye, he gave me a peck on the cheek, put his hand over his heart and said softly, "It's still in there, you know," and walked out.

The door closed behind him and I stood in the foyer, unable to move. I didn't understand what just happened, but something sure had. I walked around in a daze for the rest of that day and managed an uneasy sleep that night. The very next morning Eddie called. Before he had a chance to say anything, I said, "Eddie, I have to talk to you."

"I'll be there this afternoon."

I kept looking out of the window and heaved a sigh of relief when I saw the green jeep pull up, but I waited for him to ring the bell and come upstairs. We took one look at each other and without saying a word we were in each other's arms. I understood then what happened to me, it was Eddie. We kissed for a long time; I melted into his body like I was part of him, then pulled him towards the bedroom. He stopped me and said quietly, "I'll love you till the day I die, but I'm not leaving my wife. I have no cause."

I heard him, but at that moment I was so overwhelmed with passion, that it didn't matter. We made love in the same bed in which I shrank from him so often thirty-five years before; this time I totally surrendered. Afterwards we lay in bed reminiscing. I was surprised how many little details he remembered that I had long forgotten. He told me that his relationship with his wife no longer included sex. She had developed some female problems that caused her a lot of pain, so they now slept in separate bedrooms. But for thirty-three years she had been a good wife to him and he would not leave her. Later on, he told me that when he got home that first afternoon, Jackie had said sadly, "I guess you'll be going back to your first wife now."

Eddie's response was, "I'm not going anywhere," and to prove it, he bought her a new vacuum cleaner. I kept my mouth shut.

Eddie was seventy-one then, nine years younger than I was, and still strong, so he was able to help me. He told Jackie that I was moving away as soon as the house was sold, but that I couldn't manage the ladder to the attic He felt sorry for me, this eighty year old lady, who walked with a cane and was no longer strong enough to mow the lawn.

He came every other week with his own powerful lawn mower. It took him just twenty minutes to do the yard, then, after a lazy shower together, it was back to bed. Remembering how hard it used to be for him to turn me on, he brought a pornographic video tape one day, but I never watched it. Eddie was all I needed to turn me on. I think the intensity of my love scared him sometimes; I simply could not get enough of him, of his body, his face, his legs.

I hid a key for him outside, because he didn't always know when he could get away. I was overwhelmed when he surprised me a couple of times in the middle of the night, on his way to New Jersey to go fishing with a buddy. Usually he called me from a pay phone every other day, but there were times when I didn't hear from him for more than a week or so and I would panic—He's had a heart attack, he is in the hospital, he was in an accident, his wife found out and he can't get away any more.

Not knowing was agony. But no matter how desperate I got, I would not call him at home. Calling him might have caused him a lot of trouble. Their phone was set up, so that all incoming and outgoing calls were first recorded on the answering machine. I loved him and I didn't want to complicate his life. So, I would wait patiently for Eddie's "it's me." Eddie filled my life back then. I was so in love with him and I was grateful for every minute we spent together. I knew things would have to come to an end once I moved.

Finally, moving day arrived. Although Eddie absolutely hated driving into the city, he drove me and all my odds and ends from my home to Hallmark. But once we arrived, I couldn't even interest him in my beautiful new apartment. He was distracted and jittery and couldn't wait to leave.

Our relationship now was limited to making love over the phone. His wife usually went to the seven o'clock Mass on Sunday morning. I had an extension phone by my bed and was delighted to be woken up by his "It's me". Often it felt like he was right beside me and I wondered, why did I let him go?

For two years I lived at the Hallmark and we continued as lovers over the phone.

Then I moved to Riverdale. Even though I shared my new address once there, the phone calls stopped abruptly. For almost three years, I waited for that phone to ring on Sunday mornings, but it never did. Every green jeep I saw made my heart skip a beat, but it was never Eddie. Was he ill or even dead? His wife certainly would never let me know.

One day three years later, I called him. I left a message on their answering machine with some excuse about updating my will (I was planning to leave Eddie everything). He called back that same evening and asked, "Is something wrong?"

"Nothing is wrong, I'm updating my will and I need to know if your address is still the same."

"Nothing has changed here."

"I'm fine."

"Then why did you stop calling?" I asked.

Eddie replied, "I thought it would be better that way."

"You might have told me."

"Well, I thought you'd figure it out for yourself."

With the utmost effort I controlled my voice. "Well, take care of yourself." I hung up.

Then I burst into tears. Once the tears stopped, I was furious. Every Sunday morning for three years, I waited for that call, and then just a casual, "I'm fine." He didn't even come up with an excuse. He could have died for all I knew, but no, "he was fine," and, "Well, I thought you'd figure it out for yourself."

Those words still echo in the pit of my stomach. What a coward, I thought. He should have known that I would never do anything to endanger his marriage. For over five years I had respected his wishes and accepted the situation without complaints. No, he just was too much of a coward to face me.

Today I understand Eddie better. Not only did I take him out of his comfort zone, but I was personally too much for him. He once complained to me that he could predict every word his wife said. He felt comfortable and secure with that predictability. With her, he had blossomed and grown. With me he had felt inadequate and embarrassed. He never knew what was coming next. And let's face it, while I love being in Manhattan, taking voice lessons, painting and intently working on my autobiography, Eddie hates Manhattan.

Besides, there would be no place for him to pursue his favorite activities: gardening, working on his boat and fishing. He should have told me over the phone that he felt we couldn't make it together and that our relationship was too stressful for him. I would have understood and accepted that as I did everything else. But he couldn't face me.

I love him still and wish I could tell him how much I miss him and I believe he feels the same way. But Eddy was right, we would eventually cause each other nothing but frustration and unhappiness. I know now that it is better this way, but I still wish he should have given me the closure I so desperately needed. Three years have passed since that last phone conversation with Eddie, still while writing this and reading it over and over again, my feelings for Eddie well up with overwhelming force, even though I know it's this way is better for both of us. I ask myself:

What then is love?

Selling the House

One of the real estate agents I interviewed when I was ready to sell the house, called me right back to tell me about a family looking for a two family house on the water, just like mine. Only later did I realize that this was a trick to get me to sign on the dotted line. I fell for it and signed with him. He always gave me the feeling that he didn't like me or maybe it had to do with the run down condition of my house. I had not had the funds to have someone come in and make the house look more presentable. I was hoping a potential buyer would see beyond the cracks and the clutter, love the house, and pay the price!

A few years earlier, my downstairs office had been plundered by burglars, and I was cash poor. One night, about two weeks after installing new windows, Chris and I went out for dinner. Upon our return my neighbor came out to tell us that, when he saw someone climb through my back windows, he had called the police. The thieves were gone by the time the cops arrived and seeing nothing amiss, they just left.

I waited in the car while Chris went in to check; he came

out yelling: "They cleaned you out."

I went in to see for myself. My dog Toby lying on the living room floor, semiconscious. In the stockroom, empty plastic bins were scattered all over the place. The majority of my inventory was gone—14-carat gold jewelry worth some $300,000! Insurance was joke—the company would only cover up to $1,500 for personal jewelry in a residential area; I didn't even bother to file a claim, and I never recovered a single dollar.

The burglary was a devastating blow. I had been planning to retire right after the holiday season, and finally make a profit— but now, at seventy-two, there weren't enough years to start over and rebuild the business.

Rather than declare bankruptcy, I tried to salvage my business. I struggled to keep things afloat for another four years, but eventually, I was forced to sell. Even though I was offering a fully computerized business, it was nearly impossible to find a buyer. No one was interested in spending money for what is called 'good will' (that's everything except the merchandise). Besides, nobody wanted to work as hard as I had to make the business what it was. In the end, I sold everything for a mere $5,000. A steal for a business that should have brought $350,000, but I was too old, too tired, and too disheartened to continue.

So now, as I tried to sell my house, I couldn't afford the fix-ups required to sell quickly. Although I did as much as I could by myself, cleaning out the attic, and sorting out the clutter—I was bogged down and too overwhelmed. The house had been on the market with one agent for many months and no results, so I insisted the house be posted on a multiple listing database. This way, additional real estate agents could show the property to potential buyers—brilliant—or so I thought. As more agents began to show the house, my tenants quickly tired of the increasing visits. One day, my tenants gave one of the agents a message to rely to me: "Tell the landlady, we absolutely refuse to show the downstairs apartment any longer. Now let her try to sell the house."

At that same time, an organization developing group homes for adults with disabilities, returned for a second time and made an offer. They didn't need to see the downstairs apartment again, and they offered the asking-price. I was thrilled: a perfect situation. I was doing a *mitzvah*, a good deed, providing a home to handicapped people. There was a lot of red tape involved for the organization, so it took a couple of months before the contract was ready. After I signed it, I asked my lawyer to send a letter to the tenants, telling them the house was sold and they needed to move within sixty days. Instead, he sent them a thirty-day eviction notice! Although I assured them that the lawyer had made a mistake and they had a full sixty days to move, they refused to pay another cent in rent. I suspect they were hoping I would take them to court for non-payment. They figured they would have the opportunity to bring up an older contract and the court would force me to sell them the house for $350,000.

The group-home organization was required to notify the local community board that a group home was going to be put into the area. One of the members of that community board put a flyer in everybody's mailbox one night that read: "Gisela Selo Cohn is selling her house to a bunch of addicts and retards, who will threaten our children, bring down the value of your house and ruin our neighborhood. Be sure to attend the meeting at the school tonight to protest."

No flyer had been put in my mailbox. I found out about it that night at 10:00 p.m., when I received a telephone call from an unknown male voice that said, "I know who you sold to. I know where you're moving. You're not going to live long enough to enjoy the money you get for your house!"

Shaken, I called the police. Two hours later, they showed up and told me they could do nothing, since I didn't know who threatened me. The next day I called my lawyer about the phone call. His response was nonchalant, "Well, you knew what you were getting yourself into."

I couldn't believe it—he was supposed to be my lawyer. Why didn't he warn me before I signed the contract?

After the night of the meeting, my life became hell on earth. People gathered outside and threatened to burn the house down. I was going out; What if I returned to find slashed tires, rocks through the windows, or a swastika etched on my door.

That summer, there was a massive blackout on the East Coast. In the evenings, while every one else was catching the outside breeze, I sat alone, in the dark, and petrified. People would stop right in front of the house or across the street or even yell from their cars, "Why are you doing this to us? What did we ever do to you? Why are you punishing us?" "Money isn't everything." "Crazy, crazy!" "Why are you ruining our neighborhood?"

One night, hearing voices in the back yard, I looked out. I had not turned on a light and didn't realize I could be seen. From the pool next door, I heard repeatedly, "I see you, you fucking whore."

A few days later I received a phone call from Linda next

door. "Listen, if you can get out of that contract, I have friends who want a house on the water and will give you your asking price. They've even offered to pay any penalty involved in breaking your current contract." She paused, then added cruelly, "After all, I don't want my kids looking at retards."

I was no longer feeling up to a fight. Stress had taken it's toll and I was recovering from a recent angioplasty and two coronary stents. My blood pressure was out of control, so I decided to accept this latest offer from Linda's friends.

My doctor wrote a letter explaining that to continue with this sale would be life-threatening, and I was released from the contract with the group-home organization without a penalty. The Adovics, Linda's friends, came to see the house and loved it and I quickly received a letter of intent-to-buy from their lawyer. I figured all my troubles were over. I picked out an apartment at the Hallmark Senior Residence in downtown Manhattan and signed the lease.

Sold!

I had been waiting patiently for the Adovics to deliver a contract and a down payment for the house, but not even their lawyer returned my calls. Eventually, I called Mrs. Adovic from someone else's phone. As soon as she heard my name she hung up. I got the message.

I had not followed up on my tenants' eviction notice, because the Adovics had said they could stay on in the downstairs apartment. Just before I had to go for my first angioplasty, my tenant Joyce rang my bell. She worried that if I died while in the hospital, nobody would know that they were supposed to get reimbursed for their work downstairs, when the house was sold. So I had a codicil to my will drafted, stating that they would be entitled to $20,000 for the improvements they had made to the house and I gave them a signed and notarized copy of that codicil.

What infuriated me was that the law required me, the landlady, to provide heat and hot water and keep up the maintenance of the house and yard, even though the tenants were not paying any rent. Not only that, they never missed an opportunity to side with the neighbors.

Mike would walk down the street, waving that old invalid contract, claiming that I had gone back on my word and that they were supposed to be buying the house. Joyce, every time she saw me, asked how soon they would be getting their money and muttered that it was not nearly enough for all they did. I just referred her to my lawyer.

The situation was getting to me: the tenants, the neighbors, the endless clutter, the waiting, no money and having to pay for two residences. Right after Thanksgiving, I suddenly decided to get out of the house and move into my new apartment at the Hallmark. Unfortunately, I had advertised another tag sale for that Saturday. I figured that if I could get the movers to come on Friday and remove everything I was taking with me, whatever was left in the house was up for grabs. Since I did this on the spur of the moment, the packing boxes only arrived the day before, so when the movers arrived promptly at 8am Friday morning, I was still packing. I never got to bed that night. The tag sale was scheduled for Saturday from 9 a.m. to 5 p.m. . I had to clean up the dirt after the movers left, so it was after 10 p.m. when I started setting up the tables and putting out the merchandise. The more I shlepped, the more my back and legs hurt, and after a while I had difficulty moving at all. I was still putting on price tags when the first buyers arrived at 8 a.m.—No time to brush my teeth, wash my face, change my clothes or eat anything. A second night without sleep didn't help either. I was lucky that a couple of friends from the Senior Center came by to lend me a hand; they did all the physical work, while I handled the money. I got rid of a lot of stuff and took in about $500. Once the last customer left, I collapsed on the bed and slept for the next twelve hours. On Monday I arrived at the Hallmark, exhausted, but thrilled to be out of the house for good.

Of course I still had to get rid of all the stuff that was left in the house. That meant an hour's ride back and forth every weekend. Complicating the trip was the repair on the subway tracks in Howard Beach. Riders were shuttled to a different station, where it was necessary to climb three flights of steps just to get to the platform. Aside from aggravating my back, it added at least another half-hour to the trip each way. To avoid that, I started just staying in Howard Beach for the entire weekend. I still had my old bed, but no television, no food, and just one wooden chair. And endless clutter! My progress was incredibly slow, partly because I was now eighty, suffering from degenerated disks and spinal stenosis and partly because I was too sentimental to throw things away. The trips to Howard Beach went on for months and when it snowed, I had to go out the following day and shovel. The neighbors used to help me, but no more. Linda next door stopped by to see how I was doing and actually helped me with three more "tag sales", each one of which brought in some badly needed cash and reduced the clutter a little more. I was a physical and emotional wreck during those months.

One day, Linda made an offer on the house. Her father-in-law in Florida was not well and Sal, her husband, wanted to have his parents close by. The offer was not enough to cover the expense of the Hallmark for very long, so I turned it down.

Then I thought over my situation, I realized that I was stuck. How could I show a two-family house without including the downstairs apartment? Since the tenants refused to let me show it, I would have to evict them first. That could take months. Then I would have to be available at a moment's notice to show the house. Very difficult, now that I was living in lower Manhattan. The agent's commission would at best leave me with $525,000. So, I swallowed my pride and called Linda to tell her that I was putting the house back on the market for $575,000, but that I would let her have it for only $550,000. It worked! She called back with a counter offer of $525,000, which was just what I had hoped to make.

There was still the problem of Sal. It was Sal who a few weeks ago had called me a "fucking whore" from his pool next door. Linda had apologized for his drunken behavior at the time, but Sal had carefully avoided me ever since. I sensed that he was not a guy who would apologize for anything. Things fell into my hands—the next time he was sitting on his deck, I walked over. "Hey Sal, you owe me an apology … and I hereby accept it."

He got up, shook my hand, and gave me a big hug. He invited me in for coffee and introduced me like an old friend to his partner. The "fucking whore" incident was never mentioned. After some "important" phone calls, Sal announced magnanimously that we would be able to go to contract in a couple of weeks.

A couple of weeks later, however, he had to fly to Florida instead; his father had suffered a heart attack. Sal was gone nearly a month, and Linda couldn't continue with the sale in his absence. I worried they might be leading me on and trying to stall the sale, but, I had no choice but to wait.

My situation was desperate—I had maxed out my reverse mortgage, and I couldn't pay my rent at the Hallmark. I must say that everyone there was patient and understanding, but I was embarrassed whenever I ran into anyone from the staff.

One day Linda asked me if I would mind if Tom, Sal's partner, slept in my house during the week; on weekends he went home to his family in Florida. I said I'd think about it, but when I arrived the following Friday night, there were men's clothes all over my bedroom and a unfamiliar pillowcase. There were ashes on a newspaper on the floor by my bed. I said nothing about any of that, nor the fact that they had parked their dune buggies in my backyard and another car in my driveway. If in their minds they already owned the house, I didn't want to dislodge that thought. I did leave a note for Tom: "Please don't smoke in my bed!"

At last Linda called to tell me that the mortgage had been approved and we would be ready for the closing in a week. But Murphy's law kept pursuing me—Sal's father died and since it was a possible suicide, an inquest would be necessary before the body could be brought to New York—Sal had to stay in Florida.

I still had to clear everything out of the house. A charity organization offered to pick up the remaining furniture and household goods, including the piano. We made an appointment for the following Saturday. The day of the appointment, I arrived at the house at 10 a.m. and found Tom, practically naked, asleep in my bed. I went into the bathroom, and made a lot of noise. I was shocked to see all my towels, sopping wet, lying on the floor. Half empty coffee containers standing around everywhere and no toilet paper. I came out of the bathroom, ready to give Tom a piece of my mind, but he had left. A half hour later he came back and apologized.

He asked me if I would take fifty dollars for the be, plus the pillows, sheets, and the fan. I welcomed his offer.

Now I waited for the charity people to show up. A big truck pulled up in front of the house, I ran downstairs, relieved, but two new couches were being delivered to Mike and Joyce's apartment. Linda told me later that this was to welcome their youngest son home from jail, where he had spent the past year.

The charity organization called to tell me that their truck had broken down and they had no way to get out to Howard Beach at all. I had to find a way to empty the house. Someone put me in touch with John, a guy who sold things on eBay and he came and looked at everything. He took with him what he thought he could sell on eBay and the rest went into big black garbage bags. John had no pity, no compunctions, no sentimental attachments. I had to hold back the tears while I watched John dispose of all my carefully saved tchotchkes, but by the end of the day, those big black garbage bags stretched for half a city block, ready to be picked up by the Department of Sanitation.

The closing was scheduled twice more and twice more postponed, but was set finally for a Wednesday in August at 10:00 a.m. On the Tuesday afternoon, my lawyer left a message: "The closing is off," but at 4:00 p.m. he called back: "We're on for tomorrow after all."

As arranged, Linda picked me up at the Howard Beach subway station at 9:30 a.m. to drive to their lawyer's office in Long Island. She handed me a document; it was that old contract, but this time my signature was on it. It was forged, probably copied from the signature on the codicil I had given them. Joyce had managed to convince Linda that the contract was valid and that I couldn't sell the house to anybody else. I had to convince Linda that no one had ever signed that contract and that it was not valid. Before we headed out to Long Island, Linda had to pick up the certified check for the down payment on the house at her bank.

My lawyer was already there, drumming his fingers loudly on the table, threatening to leave, if the others weren't ready. He kept this up throughout the meeting. The amount of the bank check was incorrect and all the amounts had to be refigured. Sal kept holding up the proceeding by bringing up the money I owed the tenants, an issue that had nothing to do with the closing. Finally, all the papers got signed by all the parties, except for the down payment. That check would have to be reissued.

Linda dropped me off at the house. In my mailbox I found a seventy-five-dollar ticket from the Sanitation Department for improper recycling; something my tenants had not learned in the three-and-a-half years they lived in the house. I paid the ticket figuring that I would just deduct the cost later. Six weeks passed before I could finally bring my rent at the Hallmark up to date.

Two days after the closing Linda called. "I'm ready to sell your fucking house. Your tenants refuse to pay their rent until you give them back their security deposit."

I said I would get back to her. I took all the papers to a new lawyer. He examined the old unsigned contract-and-lease agreement, the eviction notice, and the codicil to my will. "You have no legal obligation," he said. "In fact, paying them at all would be admitting some responsibility. It's best just to forget the whole matter unless you feel a moral obligation towards the tenants. As for the codicil to your will, that will only be valid after your death."

I had no intention of obliging them with that. And moral obligation ... those people didn't know the meaning of the word "moral."

I called Linda back; reluctantly she agreed to relay all the information to Joyce. The next day there was a message on my answering machine. "This is Joyce Roccaforte. I don't care what your lawyer told you, but I'm taking you to court, and you'll end up paying plenty!"

Two months later, I was served with a summons to appear in Queens Civil Court on charges of owing money to my former tenants. The amount noted had been falsified. My instinct was to fight back, but my lawyer pointed out this would mean appearing at the Queens Court House and coming face to face with the bastards. I relented and sent a check for $4,425, only deducting $15.60 for previously owed rent and another $75 for the recycling fine. I never heard from any of them again.

More than ten years have now passed. I sometimes wonder what happened with the house and the tenants, but as they say, "Curiosity killed the cat."

The Collapse of the Wall

My sister Ingrid and I came to know each other better over the years. Joe had an office and a partner in New York City and would bring Ingrid along when he came to New York on business. I was also invited to London where they owned a fabulous house in the middle of the city in St. Johns Wood. During these visits I realized we had very little in common. Joe had become quite wealthy, and Ingrid enjoyed spending money in stores that I could not afford.

When they came to New York, Joe always managed to get theatre tickets for the three of us and we would eat in expensive restaurants. On my visits, I came to know their two boys, Antony and Stephen and shared many long talks with Denise.

When Ingrid became totally helpless, she and Joe went to live with Denise and her husband until Ingrid died of her long-time Parkinson's and shortly after that Joe's heart gave out. I kept in touch with their children via a letter that I sent out every year for the holidays.

In February of 2011, Denise emailed me that her daughter Francis was getting married in May and would I consider coming to the wedding. I decided that it was too expensive and too strenuous for me. Besides, I hardly knew Denise or her family and had no idea what kind of people they were. I had never been a very social person and to travel some eight hundred miles and end up with totally incompatible relatives was not something I wanted to do.

At the last minute, though, I changed my mind. There was nobody to represent my mother's side of the family. They were all gone: Mutti, Ingrid, Joe, and Wolfgang. So I renewed my passport, ordered a gown from one of my catalogs, and arranged the flight to London, making sure I had a wheelchair in the terminal, because my spinal stenosis and lower disk problems made walking difficult. Everything went smoothly.

At the exit from the baggage check, Denise and her husband Chris were waiting for me. I was greeted like a long lost friend with such warmth and love, the likes of which I had never experienced. Although Denise was busy with the wedding preparations, we had many a chance to talk. I was very open about the emotional problems I had suffered. Denise was completely understanding, even contributing some insight into my father's unexplainable behavior.

I shed many tears that week. But, by the time I left, I had also shed something else—my defensive wall, something I had been trying to do since I beginning psychotherapy in my early twenties. I felt that I had become a normal human being who could love and trust and get angry. It's still so new that I often feel like I'm walking on eggshells, but then, there have been occasions where I have noticed a new openness and sometimes waves of unexpected compassion. I am also more vulnerable to depression and loneliness.

At the wedding breakfast I spent a little time with each of my sister's granddaughters, and I hope to keep up that contact. I'm lazy about posting on Facebook, but I keep up with their various activities. Kirsty, one of Antony's daughters, spent a few days with me in August, and Stephen is coming with his daughter Rachel in two weeks. Sometimes I doubt that this all took place, but then I feel that new freedom that came with the collapse of the Berlin Wall. So far, it has not left me. I do notice that although I am friendly, I am rather selective about who I trust with my emotions. Sometimes I ask myself, what if I had not gone to that wedding? Without my niece, I might never have experienced love and acceptance and developed this new trust and compassion. Since that time, my personality has changed. Although I'm quite selective with whom I share my emotions, I'm much freer in my writing, my singing, and especially my painting. I'm also needier than before, perhaps age-related. I get depressed when I long for some TLC and nobody's there to give it. I would like to experience the intimacy of a close daily relationship; something I have not known in my life. Although it is unlikely to come along; I'm still always open to it. One day, I plan to make another trip to London and wallow in that wonderful feeling of being loved.

Epilogue

My ninetieth birthday made up for all the lonely birthdays I spent and all the birthday parties I never had. I felt totally loved by the world. I received so many cards, emails, phone calls, and flowers, I felt like a queen. It seemed that everybody I knew recognized me that day. The day ended with a sumptuous steak dinner in a fancy restaurant with a view of New York to which my cousin Marylou treated me. And then there was the package I received from Scotland from my great niece Kirsty; it was put together with such tender loving care that I could feel the love coming out of the package as I unpacked the photo of the two of us, beautifully framed. Included also were diabetic chocolates from Belgium, cuddle socks to keep my feet warm in bed, and a wooden massager. I was in tears as I realized with what care Kirsty put this package together. What do you give to a ninety year old? For weeks I was glowing with gratitude and love; I will never forget that wonderful feeling.

Made in the USA
Middletown, DE
20 April 2021